The Ultimate Low-Carb High-Protein Cookbook for Beginners

Simple & Delicious High-Protein Recipes to Reduce Fat and Build Lean Muscle | Includes a 30-Day Plan for an Easier Path

Liam D. Sterling

Copyright

Book Title: Low-Carb High-Protein Cookbook for Beginners

Author: Liam D. Sterling

Publication Year: 2024

All rights reserved.

This book is protected by copyright law. No part of this book may be reproduced, stored in a retrieval system, or transmitted in any form or by any means, electronic, mechanical, photocopying, recording, or otherwise, without the prior written permission of the author, except where permitted by law. For permission requests, contact the publisher or author.

Disclaimer: The information contained in this book is provided for informational purposes only and is not intended to replace the advice, diagnosis, or treatment of a qualified healthcare professional. Always consult a doctor or other qualified healthcare provider with any questions regarding a medical condition or treatment plan.

TABLE OF CONTENTS

CHAPTER 1: INTRODUCTION TO THE LOW CARB HIGH PROTEIN DIET 6

1.1 WHY A LOW CARB HIGH PROTEIN DIET? 6
   1.1.1 Benefits for Fat Loss 6
   1.1.2 Benefits for Muscle Building 6
   1.1.3 How to Sustain the Diet Long Term 7
1.2 THE SCIENCE BEHIND THE LOW CARB AND HIGH PROTEIN COMBINATION 7
   1.2.1 How Carbohydrate and Protein Metabolism Works 7
   1.2.2 The Importance of Protein for Muscle Recovery 7
   1.2.3 Reducing Carbs Without Losing Energy 8
1.3 GUIDE TO USING THIS BOOK 8
   1.3.1 How to Navigate the Recipes 8
   1.3.2 How to Adapt the Recipes for Your Goals (Fat Loss or Muscle Building) 9

CHAPTER 2: HIGH-PROTEIN BREAKFASTS 10

   Spinach & Feta High-Protein Omelette 11
   Low-Carb Protein Smoothie 12
   Chia Seed Porridge with Peanut Butter 13
   High-Protein Pancakes with Fresh Fruit 14
   High-Protein Pancakes with Fresh Fruit 15
   Egg Muffins with Vegetables 16
   Smoked Salmon and Avocado Scramble 17
   Greek Yogurt with Almonds and Berries 18
   Cottage Cheese Bowl with Seeds and Fruit 19
   Tofu Scramble with Vegetables 20
   Bacon and Egg Cups 21
   Avocado Toast with Poached Eggs 22
   Protein-Rich Breakfast Burrito 23
   Almond Flour Waffles with Blueberries 24
   Protein Oatmeal with Nuts and Seeds 25
   Scrambled Eggs with Turkey and Spinach 26

CHAPTER 3: QUICK AND BALANCED HIGH-PROTEIN LUNCHES 27

   Grilled Chicken Salad with Avocado 28
   Turkey and Spinach Wrap 29
   Beef Stir-Fry with Vegetables 30
   Tuna Salad with Quinoa and Avocado 31
   Low-Carb Zucchini Noodles with Meatballs 32
   Chicken Caesar Salad Wrap 33
   Shrimp and Avocado Salad 34
   Grilled Halloumi and Veggie Salad 35
   Salmon and Asparagus Bowl 36
   Chicken and Broccoli Stir-Fry 37
   Steak Salad with Mixed Greens 38
   Turkey Lettuce Wraps with Peanut Sauce 39
   Lentil and Chicken Soup 40
   Spaghetti Squash with Ground Beef 41
   Greek Salad with Grilled Chicken 42
   Baked Cod with Green Beans 43
   Eggplant and Ground Turkey Bake 44
   Pulled Pork Lettuce Wraps 45

Zucchini Fritters with Smoked Salmon 46

Chicken Tacos with Avocado 47

CHAPTER 4: NUTRIENT-DENSE AND FLAVORFUL DINNERS 48

Baked Salmon with Asparagus 49

Vegetable Soup with Chicken 50

Grilled Steak with Sweet Potatoes 51

Chicken Curry with Brown Rice 52

Lemon Garlic Shrimp with Cauliflower Rice 53

Baked Chicken Thighs with Brussels Sprouts 54

Lamb Chops with Spinach and Feta 55

Grilled Mackerel with Roasted Vegetables 56

Seared Tuna Steak with Broccoli 57

Turkey Meatloaf with Mashed Cauliflower 58

Eggplant Parmesan with Ground Beef 59

Roasted Duck Breast with Mushrooms 60

Pork Tenderloin with Cabbage 61

Spaghetti Squash with Pesto and Chicken 62

Chicken Fajitas with Peppers and Onions 63

Slow-Cooked Beef Stew 64

Grilled Pork Chops with Asparagus 65

Shrimp Scampi with Zoodles 66

Baked Tilapia with Spinach 67

Chicken Alfredo with Zucchini Noodles 68

CHAPTER 5: HEALTHY AND EASY-TO-MAKE SNACKS 69

Hummus and Celery Sticks 70

Hard-Boiled Eggs with Sunflower Seeds 71

Homemade Protein Bars 72

Peanut Butter Protein Shake 73

Greek Yogurt with Flax Seeds 74

Turkey Roll-Ups with Cheese 75

Cottage Cheese with Pineapple 76

Almonds and Dark Chocolate 77

Mini Caprese Skewers 78

Bell Peppers with Guacamole 79

Deviled Eggs with Avocado 80

Smoked Salmon Cucumber Bites 81

Edamame with Sea Salt 82

Cucumber and Turkey Slices 83

Protein Muffins with Berries 84

CHAPTER 6: LOW-CARB AND PROTEIN-PACKED DESSERTS 85

Chocolate Mousse with Greek Yogurt 86

Chia Seed Pudding with Coconut 87

Chocolate Protein Cake with Oats 88

Low-Carb Cheesecake 89

Almond Flour Brownies 90

Lemon Protein Bars 91

Low-Carb Chocolate Chip Cookies 92

Raspberry Protein Ice Cream 93

Peanut Butter Protein Fudge 94

Vanilla Protein Pudding 95

CHAPTER 7: MEAL PREP TIPS AND ESSENTIAL TOOLS 96

- Essential Meal Prep Tools 96
- Time-Saving Tips for Meal Prep 97

CHAPTER 8: 30-DAY MEAL PLAN GUIDE 99
- Structuring the Daily Meal Plan 99
- Balancing Protein and Carbohydrates 100
- Portion Guidelines 101
- Calorie and Macronutrient Chart 102

30-DAY MEAL PLAN FOR FAT LOSS AND MUSCLE BUILDING 105

CHAPTER 9: MAINTAINING SUCCESS AND NEXT GOALS 109
- Maintaining Results Long-Term 109
- Adapting Your Meal Plan for Future Goals 110

CONCLUSION 112

Chapter 1: Introduction to the Low Carb High Protein Diet

1.1 Why a Low Carb High Protein Diet?

Welcome! By picking up this book, you've already taken the first step toward a healthier, more active life. Whether your goal is fat loss, muscle building, or simply improving your overall well-being, adopting a Low Carb High Protein Diet can be a game changer. But why exactly is this diet so effective, and how can it fit seamlessly into your daily routine? Let's dive into that together.

A Low Carb High Protein Diet focuses on reducing the amount of carbohydrates you eat, while increasing your intake of protein-rich foods. Think of carbs as the quick-burning fuel that gives your body short bursts of energy. While they are essential in some ways, too many carbs, especially from processed foods, can lead to unwanted fat storage and energy crashes. On the other hand, protein helps build and repair muscle, keeps you fuller for longer, and supports your body's essential functions.

The beauty of this diet lies in its simplicity and flexibility. Whether you're looking to lose fat, build lean muscle, or simply feel more energized throughout the day, adjusting your protein and carb intake can bring noticeable results quickly. And don't worry – this isn't about cutting out all your favorite foods or making drastic changes overnight. The recipes and tips in this book will guide you through a balanced, sustainable approach.

1.1.1 Benefits for Fat Loss

If your primary goal is to lose weight or shed body fat, this diet is one of the most effective tools available. Here's why:

When you limit carbohydrates, your body starts to tap into its fat stores for energy, a process known as ketosis. This helps to burn fat more efficiently while stabilizing your blood sugar levels. Instead of relying on carbs for short-term energy bursts, you're training your body to become a fat-burning machine. Pretty exciting, right?

Additionally, high-protein meals are known to keep you fuller for longer. This means fewer cravings, less mindless snacking, and an easier time sticking to your caloric goals. Protein takes longer to digest than carbs, so you'll feel satisfied after meals and less likely to overeat.

A quick note here: It's important to remember that sustainable fat loss is about making manageable changes and sticking with them long-term. The recipes and meal plans we'll explore later are designed to help you achieve steady progress without feeling deprived.

1.1.2 Benefits for Muscle Building

Now, what if your goal is to build lean muscle? The Low Carb High Protein Diet is equally effective here.

Protein is the building block of muscle. Whether you're lifting weights, doing bodyweight exercises, or engaging in high-intensity interval training (HIIT), your body needs a steady supply of protein to repair and grow muscle tissue after workouts. And by limiting carbohydrates, you'll minimize the fat gain that often accompanies muscle-building diets, helping you stay lean and defined as you increase strength.

A key benefit of this diet is that it allows you to eat in a caloric surplus (which is necessary for building muscle) without overloading on unnecessary carbs. This leads to more muscle gain with minimal fat accumulation – a win-win scenario!

Throughout this book, you'll find a variety of high-protein meals specifically designed to support your muscle-building goals. Whether you're looking for a quick post-workout snack or a hearty dinner packed with protein, we've got you covered.

1.1.3 How to Sustain the Diet Long Term

At this point, you might be wondering, "This all sounds great, but how can I keep up with this diet for the long haul?" The answer is simple: balance and variety.

The Low Carb High Protein Diet isn't a short-term fix – it's a sustainable way of eating that can become part of your everyday life. By focusing on high-quality, whole-food sources of protein like chicken, fish, eggs, and plant-based options, paired with nutrient-rich vegetables and healthy fats, you'll never feel restricted or bored.

One of the keys to success is customization. Not every day will be the same, and your body's needs may change over time. That's why this book offers a variety of recipes that are easy to prepare, delicious to eat, and adaptable to different goals. You'll also learn how to adjust your meals based on whether you're focusing on fat loss or muscle building. Flexibility is the key to making this diet work for you.

By the end of this chapter, you'll have a solid understanding of how the Low Carb High Protein Diet works and why it's so effective. From here, we'll move into the science behind the combination of low carbs and high protein, giving you a deeper insight into how your body processes these nutrients.

Ready to take the next step? Let's dive into the science behind why this combination works so well!

1.2 The Science Behind the Low Carb and High Protein Combination

Now that you understand the "why" behind the Low Carb High Protein Diet, let's take a closer look at the science that makes this combination so effective. Knowledge is power, and understanding how your body processes carbs and protein will not only help you make better dietary choices but also empower you to stick with this lifestyle for the long term.

1.2.1 How Carbohydrate and Protein Metabolism Works

To fully appreciate the benefits of a Low Carb High Protein Diet, it's essential to know how your body breaks down carbohydrates and proteins.

Carbohydrates are your body's primary source of energy. When you consume carbs, your body breaks them down into glucose (sugar), which is then used for immediate energy. However, if you eat more carbs than your body needs, the excess glucose is stored as glycogen in your liver and muscles. Once these storage spaces are full, the remaining glucose is converted into fat for long-term storage. This is one of the reasons why a high-carb diet can lead to unwanted weight gain over time.

Proteins, on the other hand, play a very different role. When you eat protein-rich foods, your body breaks them down into amino acids, which are the building blocks your body uses for muscle repair, growth, and maintaining various vital functions. Unlike carbs, protein is not stored in the body for future use. It is either used immediately or excreted, which is why it's important to consume enough protein daily to support your body's needs.

When you reduce your carb intake and increase protein, you're essentially telling your body to rely more on stored fat for energy and use protein to maintain and build muscle. This is why the Low Carb High Protein Diet is so effective at burning fat while preserving lean muscle mass.

1.2.2 The Importance of Protein for Muscle Recovery

Every time you exercise—whether it's weightlifting, running, or doing yoga—you're creating tiny tears in your muscle fibers. While this might sound harmful, it's actually part of the natural process of muscle growth. After a workout, your body repairs these micro-tears, making the muscle stronger and more resilient than before. But here's the catch: this repair process requires protein.

Protein, particularly the amino acids found in it, are essential for repairing damaged muscle tissue and building new muscle. Without enough protein in your diet, your body won't have the raw materials it needs to fully recover after workouts. This can lead to muscle breakdown, fatigue, and slower progress toward your fitness goals.

That's why a high protein intake is crucial for anyone looking to build or maintain muscle, especially if you're engaging in regular physical activity. By focusing on protein-rich meals, you're ensuring that your body has everything it needs to recover efficiently, reducing muscle soreness, improving performance, and allowing you to get stronger with each workout.

1.2.3 Reducing Carbs Without Losing Energy

One of the most common concerns people have about reducing carbs is the fear of losing energy. After all, carbs are known for being the body's quick source of fuel, right? But here's the good news: your body is more adaptable than you might think!

When you reduce your carb intake, your body gradually shifts from using glucose as its main energy source to relying on fat. This process, called ketosis, allows your body to burn fat more efficiently while still maintaining steady energy levels throughout the day.

During the initial stages of a low-carb diet, you might experience a slight dip in energy, often referred to as the "keto flu." This is just your body adjusting to a new way of processing fuel. Once your metabolism adapts, you'll likely find that your energy is more stable, and those mid-afternoon energy crashes that were common on a high-carb diet become a thing of the past.

In fact, many people report feeling more energized and focused on a low-carb diet, as they're no longer experiencing the dramatic blood sugar spikes and crashes that come with high-carb meals. Your body becomes more efficient at using fat as its primary fuel source, providing you with steady, long-lasting energy.

By now, you should have a solid understanding of the science behind the Low Carb High Protein Diet. Not only does it promote fat loss by encouraging your body to burn stored fat, but it also ensures that your muscles have the protein they need to recover and grow. Plus, with your body relying on fat for fuel, you'll experience more consistent energy levels throughout the day.

Next up, we'll explore how to navigate through this book, including how to tailor the recipes to meet your specific goals—whether you're focused on fat loss or muscle building.

1.3 Guide to Using This Book

Now that you understand the core principles of the Low Carb High Protein Diet, it's time to get hands-on. This book is designed to be your go-to guide, whether you're whipping up a quick breakfast, prepping your meals for the week, or planning your 30-day journey towards fat loss or muscle building. Here's how to get the most out of it.

1.3.1 How to Navigate the Recipes

The recipes in this book are divided into different sections based on the types of meals: breakfasts, lunches, dinners, snacks, and even desserts. Each recipe is crafted to fit within the low-carb, high-protein framework, but they're far from restrictive! You'll find plenty of delicious options that are both satisfying and easy to prepare.

At the beginning of each recipe, you'll find a quick overview that includes:

- Preparation time and cooking time so you can plan your meals even when you're short on time.
- Servings for easy portion control.
- A list of ingredients that are simple to find and, in most cases, budget-friendly.

- Step-by-step instructions to guide you through the cooking process, even if you're a beginner in the kitchen.
- A breakdown of nutritional information, including calories, protein, fat, carbohydrates, and fiber per serving.

For each recipe, you'll also notice adaption tips to help you tailor the meal to your specific goals. Whether you're focusing on fat loss or building muscle, these simple tweaks will ensure the meal aligns with your personal needs.

1.3.2 How to Adapt the Recipes for Your Goals (Fat Loss or Muscle Building)

Everyone's journey is different, and this book recognizes that. That's why most recipes come with specific instructions for both fat loss and muscle building adaptations. Here's how to make sure you're getting the most out of each meal, depending on your goals:

- For Fat Loss: If your primary goal is to shed body fat, the focus will be on reducing caloric intake while maintaining protein levels to preserve muscle mass. This means you'll find adaptations that reduce the amount of fats and carbohydrates, often by substituting or minimizing ingredients like oils, high-fat cheeses, or full-fat dairy. For example, you might swap whole eggs for egg whites or use a non-stick spray instead of oil for cooking. These adjustments lower the overall calories without sacrificing the protein that's essential for muscle maintenance.
- For Muscle Building: If your goal is to build muscle, you'll need to ensure you're consuming enough calories and protein to fuel muscle growth and recovery. In the muscle-building variations, you'll see suggestions to increase protein content by adding extra eggs, lean meats, or protein-rich dairy products. Additionally, some healthy fats will be kept in the meal to provide your body with the necessary energy and to support hormone production, which is crucial for muscle growth.

Each recipe gives you the flexibility to personalize it based on where you are in your fitness journey. Whether you're looking to slim down or bulk up, there's no need to prepare separate meals or follow a completely different diet—small changes can make a big difference.

Now that you know how to navigate this book, it's time to get cooking! In the next chapters, you'll find quick and easy recipes designed to fit into your busy lifestyle. And remember, this is about progress, not perfection. Stick to your plan, make adjustments when needed, and most importantly, enjoy the process. You've got this!

Chapter 2: High-Protein Breakfasts

Breakfast is the most important meal of the day—we've all heard it before. But what's equally important is what you're eating to fuel your morning. Starting your day with a high-protein, low-carb breakfast can help you feel full, energized, and ready to take on anything, whether you're focused on fat loss or muscle building.

This section is all about quick and easy breakfast recipes that fit perfectly into a low-carb high-protein lifestyle. These meals are not only delicious, but they also give your body the fuel it needs to support your fitness goals. Whether you're getting ready for a busy day or recovering after a morning workout, these breakfasts are designed to kickstart your metabolism and keep you feeling satisfied.

We're starting with a classic: the Spinach & Feta High-Protein Omelette. This light yet satisfying meal is packed with protein and greens, making it an ideal choice for any morning. Plus, it's easy to adapt whether you're focusing on fat loss or muscle building.

Spinach & Feta High-Protein Omelette

This light yet satisfying omelette is perfect for a quick breakfast packed with protein and greens, offering a great start to your day. It's simple to customize based on your dietary goals.

Preparation Time: 5 minutes | **Cooking Time**: 10 minutes | **Servings**: 2

Ingredients:

- 4 large eggs
- 1/2 cup (60 g) fresh spinach, chopped
- 1/4 cup (60 g) feta cheese, crumbled
- 1 tablespoon (15 ml) olive oil (optional, for cooking)
- Salt and pepper to taste
- Optional: 1/4 cup (40 g) chopped cherry tomatoes

Instructions:

1. Whisk the eggs in a bowl and season with salt and pepper.
2. Heat the olive oil in a non-stick pan over medium heat.
3. Add the chopped spinach to the pan and cook for 1-2 minutes until wilted.
4. Pour the whisked eggs over the spinach, ensuring it spreads evenly.
5. Cook for about 3-4 minutes until the eggs start to set. Sprinkle feta cheese and, if desired, the chopped tomatoes on top.
6. Gently fold the omelette in half and continue cooking for another 2 minutes.
7. Serve hot, cut in half for two portions.

Nutritional Information (per serving):

Calories: 250 kcal | Protein: 17 g | Carbohydrates: 4 g | Fat: 18 g | Fiber: 1 g

Adapting for Meal Plans:

- For Fat Loss: Use only egg whites (6 egg whites instead of 4 whole eggs) and reduce the olive oil to a non-stick spray.
- For Muscle Building: Add an extra egg or 30 g of low-fat cottage cheese for additional protein.

Low-Carb Protein Smoothie

This refreshing, high-protein smoothie is an excellent option for a quick and nutritious breakfast. It's low in carbs, making it perfect for fat loss, but packed with enough protein to support muscle recovery. Customize it with your favorite low-carb fruits or toppings!

Preparation Time: 5 minutes | **Servings**: 1

Ingredients:

- 1 scoop (30 g) vanilla protein powder
- 1/2 cup (120 ml) unsweetened almond milk
- 1/4 cup (60 g) Greek yogurt
- 1/4 cup (35 g) frozen mixed berries (low-carb options like raspberries or blackberries)
- 1 tablespoon (15 g) chia seeds
- 1/4 cup (60 ml) water or ice cubes (optional, for consistency)
- Sweetener to taste (optional)

Instructions:

1. Add all the ingredients to a blender: protein powder, almond milk, Greek yogurt, frozen berries, chia seeds, and water or ice if desired.
2. Blend until smooth and creamy.
3. Taste and add a sweetener, if needed, based on your preference.
4. Pour into a glass and enjoy immediately.

Nutritional Information (per serving):

Calories: 220 kcal | Protein: 25 g | Carbohydrates: 8 g | Fat: 8 g | Fiber: 4 g

Adapting for Meal Plans:

- For Fat Loss: Use a low-fat Greek yogurt and reduce the portion of berries to lower carbs further.
- For Muscle Building: Add an extra scoop of protein powder or 1 tablespoon of peanut butter for additional protein and calories.

Chia Seed Porridge with Peanut Butter

This simple chia seed porridge is an excellent low-carb and high-protein breakfast that keeps you full for hours. Packed with fiber and healthy fats, it's perfect for starting your day or post-workout recovery.

Preparation Time: 5 minutes | **Servings**: 1

Ingredients:

- 1/4 cup (40 g) chia seeds
- 1 cup (240 ml) unsweetened almond milk
- 1 tablespoon (16 g) peanut butter
- 1 teaspoon (5 g) vanilla extract
- 1/2 teaspoon (2 g) cinnamon
- 1/4 cup (35 g) fresh berries (optional for topping)
- Sweetener to taste (optional)

Instructions:

1. In a bowl, mix the chia seeds, almond milk, vanilla extract, and cinnamon.
2. Let the mixture sit for at least 10 minutes, or refrigerate overnight for a thicker consistency. Stir occasionally to avoid clumping.
3. Once the porridge has thickened, stir in the peanut butter.
4. Top with fresh berries or any other toppings of your choice.
5. Serve chilled or at room temperature.

Nutritional Information (per serving):

Calories: 300 kcal | Protein: 12 g | Carbohydrates: 12 g | Fat: 20 g | Fiber: 10 g

Adapting for Meal Plans:

- For Fat Loss: Use powdered peanut butter to reduce fat content while maintaining flavor.
- For Muscle Building: Add 1 scoop of protein powder or extra peanut butter for an additional protein boost.

High-Protein Pancakes with Fresh Fruit

These delicious, fluffy pancakes are a perfect low-carb, high-protein breakfast option. They're easy to make and can be topped with your favorite low-carb fruits to give you a nutritious and filling start to your day.

Preparation Time: 5 minutes | **Cooking Time**: 10 minutes | **Servings**: 2

Ingredients:

- 1/2 cup (60 g) almond flour
- 1/4 cup (30 g) vanilla protein powder
- 2 large eggs
- 1/4 cup (60 ml) unsweetened almond milk
- 1 teaspoon (5 g) baking powder
- 1 teaspoon (5 g) vanilla extract
- 1/2 cup (75 g) fresh berries or fruit for topping (optional)
- Non-stick spray or butter for cooking

Instructions:

1. In a medium bowl, whisk together the almond flour, protein powder, and baking powder.
2. In another bowl, whisk the eggs, almond milk, and vanilla extract.
3. Combine the wet ingredients with the dry ingredients and stir until smooth.
4. Heat a non-stick pan over medium heat and lightly coat it with non-stick spray or butter.
5. Pour small amounts of batter into the pan to form pancakes. Cook for 2-3 minutes on each side or until golden brown.
6. Serve the pancakes topped with fresh fruit and enjoy.

Nutritional Information (per serving):

Calories: 280 kcal | Protein: 20 g | Carbohydrates: 10 g | Fat: 18 g | Fiber: 5 g

Adapting for Meal Plans:

- For Fat Loss: Use powdered peanut butter or skip the fruit topping to lower the carb content.
- For Muscle Building: Add 1 extra egg or an additional scoop of protein powder to increase protein content.

High-Protein Pancakes with Fresh Fruit

These delicious, fluffy pancakes are a perfect low-carb, high-protein breakfast option. They're easy to make and can be topped with your favorite low-carb fruits to give you a nutritious and filling start to your day.

Preparation Time: 5 minutes | **Cooking Time:** 10 minutes | **Servings:** 2

Ingredients:

- 1/2 cup (60 g) almond flour
- 1/4 cup (30 g) vanilla protein powder
- 2 large eggs
- 1/4 cup (60 ml) unsweetened almond milk
- 1 teaspoon (5 g) baking powder
- 1 teaspoon (5 g) vanilla extract
- 1/2 cup (75 g) fresh berries or fruit for topping (optional)
- Non-stick spray or butter for cooking

Instructions:

1. In a medium bowl, whisk together the almond flour, protein powder, and baking powder.
2. In another bowl, whisk the eggs, almond milk, and vanilla extract.
3. Combine the wet ingredients with the dry ingredients and stir until smooth.
4. Heat a non-stick pan over medium heat and lightly coat it with non-stick spray or butter.
5. Pour small amounts of batter into the pan to form pancakes. Cook for 2-3 minutes on each side or until golden brown.
6. Serve the pancakes topped with fresh fruit and enjoy.

Nutritional Information (per serving):

Calories: 280 kcal | Protein: 20 g | Carbohydrates: 10 g | Fat: 18 g | Fiber: 5 g

Adapting for Meal Plans:

- For Fat Loss: Use powdered peanut butter or skip the fruit topping to lower the carb content.
- For Muscle Building: Add 1 extra egg or an additional scoop of protein powder to increase protein content.

Egg Muffins with Vegetables

These protein-packed egg muffins are perfect for meal prep and make a quick, healthy breakfast that you can take on the go. They are loaded with vegetables and can be customized with different fillings based on your preference.

Preparation Time: 10 minutes | **Cooking Time**: 20 minutes | **Servings**: 6 muffins

Ingredients:

- 6 large eggs
- 1/2 cup (120 ml) unsweetened almond milk
- 1/2 cup (75 g) chopped bell peppers
- 1/4 cup (30 g) chopped spinach
- 1/4 cup (30 g) grated cheese (optional)
- 1/4 teaspoon (1 g) salt
- 1/4 teaspoon (1 g) pepper
- Non-stick spray or olive oil for greasing the muffin tin

Instructions:

1. Preheat the oven to 180°C (350°F) and lightly grease a muffin tin with non-stick spray or olive oil.
2. In a large bowl, whisk together the eggs, almond milk, salt, and pepper.
3. Stir in the chopped bell peppers, spinach, and cheese (if using).
4. Pour the egg mixture evenly into the muffin cups, filling each about 3/4 full.
5. Bake for 18-20 minutes, or until the muffins are set and lightly golden on top.
6. Let cool for a few minutes before removing from the tin. Serve warm or refrigerate for a quick grab-and-go breakfast.

Nutritional Information (per muffin):

Calories: 90 kcal | Protein: 8 g | Carbohydrates: 2 g | Fat: 6 g | Fiber: 1 g

Adapting for Meal Plans:

- For Fat Loss: Use egg whites instead of whole eggs to reduce fat content.
- For Muscle Building: Add 1/4 cup (30 g) diced cooked turkey sausage or ham for extra protein.

Smoked Salmon and Avocado Scramble

This rich and creamy scrambled egg dish combines the healthy fats from avocado with the lean protein from smoked salmon, making it a perfect low-carb, high-protein breakfast that's both delicious and nutritious.

Preparation Time: 5 minutes | **Cooking Time**: 5 minutes | **Servings**: 2

Ingredients:

- 4 large eggs
- 1/4 cup (60 ml) unsweetened almond milk
- 100 g smoked salmon, sliced
- 1/2 avocado, diced
- 1 tablespoon (15 ml) olive oil or butter
- Salt and pepper to taste
- Fresh chives for garnish (optional)

Instructions:

1. In a bowl, whisk the eggs and almond milk together, seasoning with salt and pepper.
2. Heat olive oil or butter in a non-stick pan over medium heat.
3. Pour the egg mixture into the pan and cook gently, stirring occasionally until softly scrambled.
4. Add the smoked salmon and avocado pieces, folding them into the eggs just before they finish cooking.
5. Remove from heat and serve immediately, garnished with fresh chives if desired.

Nutritional Information (per serving):

Calories: 320 kcal | Protein: 22 g | Carbohydrates: 4 g | Fat: 25 g | Fiber: 3 g

Adapting for Meal Plans:

- For Fat Loss: Use egg whites in place of whole eggs and reduce the portion of avocado to lower fat content.
- For Muscle Building: Add an extra egg or 2 tablespoons of cottage cheese for additional protein.

Greek Yogurt with Almonds and Berries

This simple yet delicious breakfast combines creamy Greek yogurt with crunchy almonds and fresh berries, offering a high-protein, low-carb start to your day. It's quick to prepare and packed with nutrients to keep you energized.

Preparation Time: 5 minutes | **Servings**: 1

Ingredients:

- 1 cup (240 g) plain Greek yogurt (full-fat or low-fat)
- 1/4 cup (30 g) almonds, chopped
- 1/4 cup (35 g) fresh berries (raspberries, blueberries, or strawberries)
- 1 tablespoon (10 g) chia seeds or flaxseeds (optional)
- 1 teaspoon (5 g) honey or sweetener of choice (optional)

Instructions:

1. In a bowl, add the Greek yogurt and top with the chopped almonds and fresh berries.
2. Sprinkle chia seeds or flaxseeds on top for extra fiber (optional).
3. Drizzle with honey or your preferred sweetener, if desired.
4. Stir gently and enjoy immediately.

Nutritional Information (per serving):

Calories: 280 kcal | Protein: 20 g | Carbohydrates: 14 g | Fat: 15 g | Fiber: 5 g

Adapting for Meal Plans:

- For Fat Loss: Use low-fat Greek yogurt and reduce the quantity of almonds for lower fat content.
- For Muscle Building: Add 1 scoop of protein powder or an extra serving of almonds for increased protein and healthy fats.

Cottage Cheese Bowl with Seeds and Fruit

This protein-packed breakfast is simple to prepare and provides a satisfying mix of creamy cottage cheese, crunchy seeds, and sweet fresh fruit. It's perfect for those looking for a nutritious and quick meal to start the day.

Preparation Time: 5 minutes | **Servings**: 1

Ingredients:

- 1 cup (240 g) cottage cheese (low-fat or full-fat)
- 1/4 cup (35 g) fresh fruit (berries, apple slices, or peaches)
- 1 tablespoon (10 g) pumpkin or sunflower seeds
- 1 teaspoon (5 g) chia seeds or flaxseeds (optional)
- 1 teaspoon (5 g) honey or sweetener of choice (optional)

Instructions:

1. Place the cottage cheese in a bowl and top with your choice of fresh fruit.
2. Sprinkle pumpkin or sunflower seeds on top, followed by chia seeds or flaxseeds if desired.
3. Drizzle with honey or sweetener of choice for extra sweetness, if desired.
4. Mix gently and enjoy immediately.

Nutritional Information (per serving):

Calories: 250 kcal | Protein: 20 g | Carbohydrates: 12 g | Fat: 10 g | Fiber: 4 g

Adapting for Meal Plans:

- For Fat Loss: Use low-fat cottage cheese and reduce the amount of seeds to lower fat content.
- For Muscle Building: Add 1 scoop of protein powder or an extra serving of seeds for increased protein and healthy fats.

Tofu Scramble with Vegetables

This tofu scramble is a plant-based, protein-rich alternative to traditional scrambled eggs. Packed with vegetables and full of flavor, it's a perfect option for a nutritious, low-carb, high-protein breakfast.

Preparation Time: 5 minutes | **Cooking Time:** 10 minutes | **Servings:** 2

Ingredients:

- 200 g firm tofu, drained and crumbled
- 1/2 cup (75 g) bell peppers, chopped
- 1/4 cup (30 g) spinach, chopped
- 1/4 cup (30 g) onion, finely diced
- 1 tablespoon (15 ml) olive oil
- 1/2 teaspoon (2 g) turmeric (optional for color)
- Salt and pepper to taste
- Fresh herbs for garnish (optional)

Instructions:

1. Heat the olive oil in a non-stick pan over medium heat.
2. Add the onions and bell peppers, cooking for 3-4 minutes until softened.
3. Crumble the tofu into the pan, adding the turmeric, salt, and pepper. Stir well to combine.
4. Cook for 4-5 minutes, stirring occasionally, until the tofu is heated through and slightly browned.
5. Add the spinach and cook for another 1-2 minutes until wilted.
6. Garnish with fresh herbs, if desired, and serve immediately.

Nutritional Information (per serving):

Calories: 180 kcal | Protein: 15 g | Carbohydrates: 6 g | Fat: 10 g | Fiber: 3 g

Adapting for Meal Plans:

- For Fat Loss: Reduce the olive oil to a non-stick spray to lower fat content.
- For Muscle Building: Add 1/4 cup (40 g) of black beans or chickpeas for additional protein and fiber.

Bacon and Egg Cups

These bacon and egg cups are a quick, easy, and portable breakfast option. Packed with protein and healthy fats, they're a perfect low-carb start to your day and can be prepped ahead for busy mornings.

Preparation Time: 5 minutes | **Cooking Time**: 15 minutes | **Servings**: 6 cups

Ingredients:

- 6 large eggs
- 6 slices of bacon
- Salt and pepper to taste
- Optional: 1/4 cup (30 g) shredded cheese
- Fresh herbs for garnish (optional)

Instructions:

1. Preheat the oven to 180°C (350°F) and grease a muffin tin.
2. Cook the bacon slices in a pan until they're partially cooked but still pliable.
3. Line each muffin cup with one slice of bacon, creating a "cup" shape.
4. Crack one egg into each bacon-lined cup. Season with salt and pepper, and add cheese if desired.
5. Bake for 12-15 minutes, or until the eggs are set to your preferred doneness.
6. Remove from the oven and garnish with fresh herbs if desired. Serve warm.

Nutritional Information (per cup):

Calories: 140 kcal | Protein: 10 g | Carbohydrates: 1 g | Fat: 11 g | Fiber: 0 g

Adapting for Meal Plans:

- For Fat Loss: Use turkey bacon to reduce fat content.
- For Muscle Building: Add an extra egg white per cup or top with cheese for more protein.

Avocado Toast with Poached Eggs

This popular and nutritious breakfast pairs creamy avocado with perfectly poached eggs on a low-carb bread base, making it a delicious and protein-rich start to your day.

Preparation Time: 5 minutes | **Cooking Time:** 5 minutes | **Servings:** 1

Ingredients:

- 1 slice low-carb bread (or any whole-grain bread)
- 1/2 avocado, mashed
- 2 large eggs
- 1 tablespoon (15 ml) vinegar (for poaching)
- Salt and pepper to taste
- Optional: red pepper flakes or fresh herbs for garnish

Instructions:

1. Toast the slice of bread and spread the mashed avocado evenly on top.
2. To poach the eggs: Bring a small pot of water to a gentle simmer. Add the vinegar to the water.
3. Crack the eggs into a cup and gently lower them into the simmering water. Cook for 3-4 minutes or until the whites are set and the yolk is still runny.
4. Use a slotted spoon to remove the poached eggs from the water and place them on top of the avocado toast.
5. Season with salt, pepper, and red pepper flakes or fresh herbs if desired. Serve immediately.

Nutritional Information (per serving):

Calories: 350 kcal | Protein: 14 g | Carbohydrates: 18 g | Fat: 24 g | Fiber: 8 g

Adapting for Meal Plans:

- For Fat Loss: Use only egg whites to lower calorie and fat content.
- For Muscle Building: Add an extra egg or 1 slice of turkey bacon for additional protein.

Protein-Rich Breakfast Burrito

This high-protein breakfast burrito is a perfect grab-and-go option for busy mornings. It's loaded with eggs, lean meat, and vegetables, all wrapped in a low-carb tortilla for a balanced and satisfying meal.

Preparation Time: 10 minutes | **Cooking Time**: 10 minutes | **Servings**: 1

Ingredients:

- 2 large eggs
- 1/4 cup (60 g) cooked chicken or turkey breast, diced
- 1/4 cup (30 g) bell peppers, chopped
- 1/4 cup (30 g) spinach, chopped
- 1 low-carb tortilla
- 1 tablespoon (15 g) salsa (optional)
- 1 tablespoon (15 g) shredded cheese (optional)
- Salt and pepper to taste
- Non-stick spray for cooking

Instructions:

1. Heat a non-stick pan over medium heat and lightly coat with non-stick spray.
2. Whisk the eggs in a bowl, then add to the pan, cooking until scrambled. Season with salt and pepper.
3. Add the diced chicken or turkey, bell peppers, and spinach to the eggs. Stir until the vegetables are tender and the eggs are fully cooked.
4. Warm the low-carb tortilla in a separate pan or microwave.
5. Place the egg mixture in the center of the tortilla. Top with salsa and shredded cheese if desired.
6. Roll the tortilla into a burrito and serve immediately.

Nutritional Information (per serving):

Calories: 320 kcal | Protein: 25 g | Carbohydrates: 10 g | Fat: 18 g | Fiber: 5 g

Adapting for Meal Plans:

- For Fat Loss: Use egg whites instead of whole eggs and skip the cheese.
- For Muscle Building: Add an extra egg or double the portion of chicken/turkey for more protein.

Almond Flour Waffles with Blueberries

These light and fluffy almond flour waffles are a low-carb, high-protein breakfast option that's perfect for a weekend treat. Top them with fresh blueberries for an extra burst of flavor and nutrients.

Preparation Time: 5 minutes | **Cooking Time:** 10 minutes | **Servings:** 2

Ingredients:

- 1 cup (120 g) almond flour
- 1/4 cup (30 g) vanilla protein powder
- 2 large eggs
- 1/4 cup (60 ml) unsweetened almond milk
- 1 tablespoon (15 ml) melted coconut oil
- 1 teaspoon (5 g) baking powder
- 1/2 teaspoon (2 g) vanilla extract
- 1/2 cup (75 g) fresh blueberries (for topping)
- Non-stick spray for waffle iron

Instructions:

1. Preheat your waffle iron and lightly grease it with non-stick spray.
2. In a bowl, whisk together the almond flour, protein powder, and baking powder.
3. In another bowl, beat the eggs, almond milk, coconut oil, and vanilla extract.
4. Combine the wet and dry ingredients, stirring until smooth.
5. Pour the batter into the waffle iron and cook according to the manufacturer's instructions until the waffles are golden and crisp.
6. Serve the waffles topped with fresh blueberries.

Nutritional Information (per serving):

Calories: 350 kcal | Protein: 20 g | Carbohydrates: 12 g | Fat: 28 g | Fiber: 6 g

Adapting for Meal Plans:

- For Fat Loss: Reduce the portion of coconut oil or skip the blueberries to lower calories and fat.
- For Muscle Building: Add an extra scoop of protein powder or serve with a side of Greek yogurt for additional protein.

Protein Oatmeal with Nuts and Seeds

This warm and filling protein oatmeal is a great way to start your day. Packed with fiber, healthy fats, and protein, it's customizable with your favorite nuts and seeds, making it perfect for any meal plan.

Preparation Time: 5 minutes | **Cooking Time**: 5 minutes | **Servings**: 1

Ingredients:

- 1/2 cup (40 g) rolled oats
- 1 scoop (30 g) vanilla protein powder
- 1 cup (240 ml) unsweetened almond milk or water
- 1 tablespoon (15 g) chia seeds or flaxseeds
- 1 tablespoon (10 g) almonds, chopped
- 1 tablespoon (10 g) walnuts, chopped
- 1 teaspoon (5 g) cinnamon
- Optional: Fresh fruit or honey for topping

Instructions:

1. In a small saucepan, bring the almond milk or water to a boil. Add the oats and reduce the heat to a simmer, cooking for 3-4 minutes.
2. Stir in the protein powder, chia seeds or flaxseeds, and cinnamon. Cook for an additional 1-2 minutes until the mixture thickens.
3. Remove from heat and top with the chopped almonds, walnuts, and any optional toppings like fresh fruit or honey.
4. Serve warm.

Nutritional Information (per serving):

Calories: 350 kcal | Protein: 22 g | Carbohydrates: 35 g | Fat: 15 g | Fiber: 8 g

Adapting for Meal Plans:

- For Fat Loss: Use water instead of almond milk and reduce the portion of nuts to lower the fat and calorie content.
- For Muscle Building: Add an extra scoop of protein powder or top with Greek yogurt for more protein.

Scrambled Eggs with Turkey and Spinach

This high-protein breakfast combines fluffy scrambled eggs with lean turkey and nutrient-rich spinach. It's a quick, low-carb option that will keep you full and energized throughout the morning.

Preparation Time: 5 minutes | **Cooking Time:** 5 minutes | **Servings:** 2

Ingredients:

- 4 large eggs
- 1/4 cup (60 g) cooked turkey breast, diced
- 1 cup (30 g) fresh spinach, chopped
- 1 tablespoon (15 ml) olive oil or butter
- Salt and pepper to taste
- Optional: shredded cheese for topping

Instructions:

1. Heat the olive oil or butter in a non-stick pan over medium heat.
2. Add the spinach and cook for 1-2 minutes until wilted.
3. In a bowl, whisk the eggs and season with salt and pepper.
4. Pour the eggs into the pan with the spinach, stirring gently.
5. Add the diced turkey and cook until the eggs are fully scrambled and set.
6. Top with shredded cheese if desired and serve warm.

Nutritional Information (per serving):

Calories: 250 kcal | Protein: 20 g | Carbohydrates: 3 g | Fat: 18 g | Fiber: 1 g

Adapting for Meal Plans:

- For Fat Loss: Use egg whites instead of whole eggs and reduce or omit the olive oil.
- For Muscle Building: Add an extra egg or top with extra cheese for additional protein and calories.

Chapter 3: Quick and Balanced High-Protein Lunches

Lunch is an essential meal to keep you energized and focused throughout the day. Whether you're at work, running errands, or squeezing in a workout, having a balanced, high-protein lunch ensures you stay full and fueled until your next meal. A well-planned lunch can prevent energy crashes, keep cravings at bay, and help you stick to your low-carb, high-protein diet with ease.

In this section, you'll find a collection of quick and easy lunches that are perfect for busy weekdays. These meals are designed to give you the nutrients you need, without spending hours in the kitchen. Whether you're focusing on fat loss or muscle building, each recipe is easily adaptable to fit your fitness goals.

We'll kick off with a refreshing Grilled Chicken Salad with Avocado. This versatile dish is packed with lean protein and healthy fats, making it a great option for both fat loss and muscle building.

Grilled Chicken Salad with Avocado

This light yet satisfying grilled chicken salad is packed with lean protein and healthy fats from avocado. It's a perfect low-carb lunch that can be easily adjusted based on your fitness goals.

Preparation Time: 10 minutes | **Cooking Time**: 15 minutes | **Servings**: 2

Ingredients:

- 200 g grilled chicken breast, sliced
- 4 cups (120 g) mixed salad greens
- 1 avocado, sliced
- 1/4 cup (60 g) cherry tomatoes, halved
- 1/4 cup (60 g) cucumber, sliced
- 1 tablespoon (15 ml) olive oil
- 1 tablespoon (15 ml) lemon juice
- Salt and pepper to taste
- Optional: 1 tablespoon (15 g) sunflower seeds or pumpkin seeds

Instructions:

1. In a large bowl, toss the salad greens, cherry tomatoes, cucumber, and avocado.
2. Top with the grilled chicken slices.
3. Drizzle with olive oil and lemon juice, and season with salt and pepper.
4. Sprinkle with sunflower or pumpkin seeds if desired and serve immediately.

Nutritional Information (per serving):

Calories: 400 kcal | Protein: 35 g | Carbohydrates: 12 g | Fat: 25 g | Fiber: 8 g

Adapting for Meal Plans:

- For Fat Loss: Use only half an avocado and reduce the olive oil to lower fat content.
- For Muscle Building: Add an extra 100 g of grilled chicken and top with extra seeds for more protein and healthy fats.

Turkey and Spinach Wrap

This quick and easy turkey and spinach wrap is perfect for a busy day when you need a satisfying, protein-packed meal. With lean turkey and fresh spinach, it's a balanced, low-carb lunch that you can take on the go.

Preparation Time: 5 minutes | **Cooking Time**: None | **Servings**: 1

Ingredients:

- 100 g cooked turkey breast, sliced
- 1 low-carb wrap or tortilla
- 1/2 cup (15 g) fresh spinach leaves
- 2 tablespoons (30 g) hummus or Greek yogurt
- 1/4 cup (60 g) cucumber slices
- 1/4 cup (60 g) bell pepper slices
- Salt and pepper to taste

Instructions:

1. Spread the hummus or Greek yogurt evenly over the low-carb wrap.
2. Layer the spinach, turkey breast, cucumber, and bell pepper slices on top.
3. Season with salt and pepper to taste.
4. Roll the wrap tightly, slice in half, and enjoy immediately or wrap it up for later.

Nutritional Information (per serving):

Calories: 280 kcal | Protein: 25 g | Carbohydrates: 15 g | Fat: 10 g | Fiber: 6 g

Adapting for Meal Plans:

- For Fat Loss: Use a lower-calorie hummus or Greek yogurt and reduce the portion size of the wrap.
- For Muscle Building: Add an extra 50 g of turkey or a slice of cheese for additional protein.

Beef Stir-Fry with Vegetables

This quick and flavorful beef stir-fry is a perfect high-protein, low-carb lunch. Packed with lean beef and fresh vegetables, it's both nutritious and satisfying, making it ideal for muscle building or fat loss.

Preparation Time: 10 minutes | **Cooking Time**: 10 minutes | **Servings**: 2

Ingredients:

- 200 g lean beef strips
- 1 tablespoon (15 ml) olive oil
- 1 cup (150 g) broccoli florets
- 1/2 cup (75 g) bell peppers, sliced
- 1/4 cup (30 g) carrots, julienned
- 2 tablespoons (30 ml) soy sauce or tamari
- 1 teaspoon (5 g) ginger, minced
- 1 garlic clove, minced
- Optional: sesame seeds for garnish

Instructions:

1. Heat the olive oil in a large pan or wok over medium-high heat.
2. Add the beef strips and cook for 2-3 minutes until browned. Remove from the pan and set aside.
3. In the same pan, add the broccoli, bell peppers, and carrots. Stir-fry for 3-4 minutes until tender but still crisp.
4. Add the garlic and ginger, and cook for another minute.
5. Return the beef to the pan and stir in the soy sauce or tamari. Cook for another 2 minutes, stirring occasionally.
6. Serve hot, garnished with sesame seeds if desired.

Nutritional Information (per serving):

Calories: 350 kcal | Protein: 30 g | Carbohydrates: 10 g | Fat: 20 g | Fiber: 4 g

Adapting for Meal Plans:

- For Fat Loss: Use leaner cuts of beef, such as sirloin, and reduce the olive oil to a non-stick spray.
- For Muscle Building: Add 1/2 cup (75 g) of cooked quinoa or brown rice for extra carbohydrates and calories.

Tuna Salad with Quinoa and Avocado

This tuna salad with quinoa and avocado is a nutrient-packed lunch option. It's rich in protein, healthy fats, and complex carbohydrates, making it ideal for sustained energy and muscle recovery.

Preparation Time: 10 minutes | **Cooking Time**: 15 minutes (for quinoa) | **Servings**: 2

Ingredients:

- 1 can (150 g) tuna in water, drained
- 1/2 cup (85 g) cooked quinoa
- 1 avocado, diced
- 1/4 cup (60 g) cherry tomatoes, halved
- 1/4 cup (60 g) cucumber, diced
- 2 tablespoons (30 ml) olive oil
- 1 tablespoon (15 ml) lemon juice
- Salt and pepper to taste
- Optional: fresh parsley or cilantro for garnish

Instructions:

1. In a large bowl, combine the cooked quinoa, drained tuna, avocado, cherry tomatoes, and cucumber.
2. Drizzle with olive oil and lemon juice.
3. Season with salt and pepper, and mix well.
4. Garnish with fresh parsley or cilantro if desired, and serve.

Nutritional Information (per serving):

Calories: 450 kcal | Protein: 30 g | Carbohydrates: 22 g | Fat: 28 g | Fiber: 10 g

Adapting for Meal Plans:

- For Fat Loss: Use only half the avocado and reduce the olive oil to 1 tablespoon.
- For Muscle Building: Add an extra 1/4 cup (45 g) of quinoa for more carbohydrates and calories.

Low-Carb Zucchini Noodles with Meatballs

This low-carb version of a classic dish replaces traditional pasta with zucchini noodles, paired with delicious, high-protein meatballs. It's a perfect meal for those looking to keep carbs low while enjoying a hearty and satisfying lunch.

Preparation Time: 15 minutes | **Cooking Time:** 20 minutes | **Servings:** 2

Ingredients:

- 2 medium zucchinis, spiralized into noodles
- 200 g ground beef or turkey
- 1/4 cup (30 g) grated Parmesan cheese (optional)
- 1 egg
- 1/4 cup (30 g) breadcrumbs (or almond flour for a low-carb option)
- 1/2 teaspoon (2 g) garlic powder
- 1/2 teaspoon (2 g) onion powder
- Salt and pepper to taste
- 1 tablespoon (15 ml) olive oil
- 1 cup (240 ml) marinara sauce (low-sugar)

Instructions:

1. Preheat the oven to 180°C (350°F).
2. In a bowl, combine the ground beef or turkey, egg, Parmesan, breadcrumbs or almond flour, garlic powder, onion powder, salt, and pepper. Mix well.
3. Form the mixture into small meatballs and place them on a baking sheet. Bake for 15-20 minutes until cooked through.
4. While the meatballs are baking, heat the olive oil in a large pan and sauté the zucchini noodles for 2-3 minutes until slightly softened.
5. Warm the marinara sauce in a separate pan.
6. Serve the meatballs over the zucchini noodles, topped with marinara sauce. Enjoy!

Nutritional Information (per serving):

Calories: 380 kcal | Protein: 28 g | Carbohydrates: 12 g | Fat: 25 g | Fiber: 4 g

Adapting for Meal Plans:

- For Fat Loss: Use lean turkey and skip the Parmesan and breadcrumbs to reduce fat and calories.
- For Muscle Building: Use beef and add extra Parmesan or a sprinkle of cheese on top for additional protein and calories.

Chicken Caesar Salad Wrap

This Chicken Caesar Salad Wrap is a delicious, portable version of the classic Caesar salad. It's packed with lean protein and healthy fats, making it an ideal low-carb lunch option.

Preparation Time: 10 minutes | **Cooking Time**: None | **Servings**: 1

Ingredients:

- 100 g cooked chicken breast, sliced
- 1 low-carb tortilla or wrap
- 1/2 cup (30 g) chopped romaine lettuce
- 1 tablespoon (15 g) grated Parmesan cheese
- 2 tablespoons (30 ml) Caesar dressing (low-fat or regular)
- Salt and pepper to taste
- Optional: 1 tablespoon (15 g) croutons for added crunch

Instructions:

1. Lay the tortilla flat and spread the Caesar dressing evenly over it.
2. Layer the romaine lettuce, chicken breast slices, and Parmesan cheese on top.
3. Season with salt and pepper to taste.
4. Roll the tortilla tightly to form a wrap, slice in half, and serve immediately or pack for later.

Nutritional Information (per serving):

Calories: 350 kcal | Protein: 28 g | Carbohydrates: 12 g | Fat: 20 g | Fiber: 5 g

Adapting for Meal Plans:

- For Fat Loss: Use a low-fat Caesar dressing and skip the Parmesan and croutons.
- For Muscle Building: Add an extra 50 g of chicken or a slice of bacon for more protein.

Shrimp and Avocado Salad

This refreshing shrimp and avocado salad is a light yet filling option, rich in protein and healthy fats. It's perfect for a quick, low-carb lunch that's both delicious and nutritious.

Preparation Time: 10 minutes | **Cooking Time**: 5 minutes | **Servings**: 2

Ingredients:

- 200 g shrimp, peeled and deveined
- 1 tablespoon (15 ml) olive oil
- 1 avocado, diced
- 2 cups (60 g) mixed greens
- 1/2 cup (60 g) cucumber, diced
- 1/4 cup (60 g) cherry tomatoes, halved
- 1 tablespoon (15 ml) lemon juice
- Salt and pepper to taste
- Optional: 1 tablespoon (15 g) feta cheese for topping

Instructions:

1. Heat the olive oil in a pan over medium heat. Add the shrimp and cook for 3-4 minutes, until pink and cooked through. Season with salt and pepper.
2. In a large bowl, combine the mixed greens, cucumber, cherry tomatoes, and avocado.
3. Add the cooked shrimp and drizzle with lemon juice. Toss gently to combine.
4. Top with feta cheese if desired and serve immediately.

Nutritional Information (per serving):

Calories: 350 kcal | Protein: 25 g | Carbohydrates: 10 g | Fat: 24 g | Fiber: 8 g

Adapting for Meal Plans:

- For Fat Loss: Use only half an avocado and reduce the olive oil to lower fat content.
- For Muscle Building: Add extra shrimp or top with 1/4 cup (30 g) of quinoa for additional protein and carbohydrates.

Grilled Halloumi and Veggie Salad

This Grilled Halloumi and Veggie Salad is a savory, high-protein meal that's rich in flavor and perfect for a quick lunch. Halloumi cheese provides a unique texture and taste, while the fresh vegetables keep the dish light and healthy.

Preparation Time: 10 minutes | **Cooking Time**: 10 minutes | **Servings**: 2

Ingredients:

- 200 g halloumi cheese, sliced
- 1 tablespoon (15 ml) olive oil
- 2 cups (60 g) mixed greens
- 1/2 cup (60 g) cherry tomatoes, halved
- 1/2 cup (75 g) zucchini, thinly sliced
- 1/4 cup (60 g) red bell pepper, sliced
- 1 tablespoon (15 ml) balsamic vinegar
- Salt and pepper to taste
- Optional: fresh herbs for garnish

Instructions:

1. Heat the olive oil in a grill pan or regular pan over medium heat. Grill the halloumi slices for 2-3 minutes on each side, until golden brown. Remove from heat.
2. In the same pan, lightly grill the zucchini and red bell pepper for 2-3 minutes until softened.
3. In a large bowl, combine the mixed greens, cherry tomatoes, and grilled vegetables.
4. Top with grilled halloumi slices and drizzle with balsamic vinegar. Season with salt and pepper.
5. Garnish with fresh herbs if desired, and serve immediately.

Nutritional Information (per serving):

Calories: 400 kcal | Protein: 22 g | Carbohydrates: 10 g | Fat: 30 g | Fiber: 4 g

Adapting for Meal Plans:

- For Fat Loss: Reduce the amount of halloumi to 100 g and use a non-stick spray instead of olive oil.
- For Muscle Building: Add an extra 100 g of halloumi or top with grilled chicken for more protein.

Salmon and Asparagus Bowl

This simple yet delicious salmon and asparagus bowl is packed with lean protein and essential fats. It's a perfect low-carb, high-protein lunch that's light, flavorful, and easy to prepare.

Preparation Time: 10 minutes | **Cooking Time**: 15 minutes | **Servings**: 2

Ingredients:

- 200 g salmon fillet
- 1 tablespoon (15 ml) olive oil
- 1 bunch (200 g) asparagus, trimmed
- 2 cups (60 g) mixed greens
- 1/4 cup (60 g) cherry tomatoes, halved
- 1 tablespoon (15 ml) lemon juice
- Salt and pepper to taste
- Optional: fresh dill for garnish

Instructions:

1. Preheat the oven to 180°C (350°F).
2. Place the salmon fillet on a baking sheet and drizzle with half of the olive oil. Season with salt, pepper, and lemon juice.
3. Roast the salmon in the oven for 12-15 minutes, until fully cooked and flaky.
4. While the salmon is baking, heat the remaining olive oil in a pan over medium heat. Add the asparagus and sauté for 4-5 minutes, until tender.
5. In a bowl, combine the mixed greens, cherry tomatoes, and cooked asparagus.
6. Top with the baked salmon fillet, garnish with fresh dill if desired, and serve.

Nutritional Information (per serving):

Calories: 420 kcal | Protein: 35 g | Carbohydrates: 10 g | Fat: 28 g | Fiber: 5 g

Adapting for Meal Plans:

- For Fat Loss: Use only 1/2 tablespoon of olive oil and reduce the portion of salmon to 150 g to lower calorie content.
- For Muscle Building: Increase the portion of salmon to 300 g and add 1/2 cup (75 g) of quinoa for extra protein and carbohydrates.

Chicken and Broccoli Stir-Fry

This quick and flavorful chicken and broccoli stir-fry is a perfect high-protein, low-carb lunch option. Packed with lean chicken and fresh broccoli, it's a simple, nutritious meal that's ideal for busy days.

Preparation Time: 10 minutes | **Cooking Time**: 10 minutes | **Servings**: 2

Ingredients:

- 200 g chicken breast, sliced into strips
- 1 tablespoon (15 ml) olive oil
- 2 cups (150 g) broccoli florets
- 1/4 cup (60 ml) low-sodium soy sauce or tamari
- 1 teaspoon (5 g) ginger, minced
- 1 garlic clove, minced
- 1/4 teaspoon (1 g) red pepper flakes (optional)
- 1/4 cup (60 ml) chicken broth (optional, for extra sauce)
- Optional: sesame seeds for garnish

Instructions:

1. Heat the olive oil in a large pan or wok over medium-high heat.
2. Add the chicken strips and cook for 5-6 minutes until golden brown and cooked through. Remove from the pan and set aside.
3. In the same pan, add the broccoli florets and stir-fry for 3-4 minutes until tender but still crisp.
4. Add the garlic, ginger, and red pepper flakes (if using) to the broccoli. Cook for 1 minute.
5. Return the chicken to the pan and stir in the soy sauce and chicken broth (if using). Cook for another 2-3 minutes, stirring occasionally.
6. Serve hot, garnished with sesame seeds if desired.

Nutritional Information (per serving):

Calories: 300 kcal | Protein: 35 g | Carbohydrates: 8 g | Fat: 15 g | Fiber: 4 g

Adapting for Meal Plans:

- For Fat Loss: Use less olive oil and opt for skinless chicken breast to reduce fat content.
- For Muscle Building: Add 1/2 cup (75 g) of cooked quinoa or brown rice for extra carbohydrates and calories.

Steak Salad with Mixed Greens

This hearty steak salad combines lean protein from the steak with fresh mixed greens and colorful vegetables. It's a satisfying, low-carb lunch that's full of flavor and nutrients.

Preparation Time: 10 minutes | **Cooking Time**: 10 minutes | **Servings**: 2

Ingredients:

- 200 g lean steak (sirloin or flank)
- 1 tablespoon (15 ml) olive oil
- 4 cups (120 g) mixed salad greens
- 1/2 cup (60 g) cherry tomatoes, halved
- 1/4 cup (60 g) cucumber, sliced
- 1/4 cup (30 g) red onion, thinly sliced
- 1 tablespoon (15 ml) balsamic vinegar
- Salt and pepper to taste
- Optional: 1 tablespoon (15 g) feta cheese or blue cheese

Instructions:

1. Heat the olive oil in a grill pan or regular pan over medium-high heat. Season the steak with salt and pepper, and grill for 4-5 minutes on each side, or until it reaches your desired level of doneness. Let the steak rest for a few minutes before slicing it thinly.
2. In a large bowl, toss the mixed greens, cherry tomatoes, cucumber, and red onion.
3. Top the salad with the sliced steak and drizzle with balsamic vinegar.
4. Add feta or blue cheese for extra flavor if desired, and serve immediately.

Nutritional Information (per serving):

Calories: 400 kcal | Protein: 35 g | Carbohydrates: 10 g | Fat: 25 g | Fiber: 4 g

Adapting for Meal Plans:

- For Fat Loss: Use a leaner cut of steak and reduce or omit the cheese.
- For Muscle Building: Increase the portion of steak to 300 g and add extra cheese for additional protein and calories.

Turkey Lettuce Wraps with Peanut Sauce

These turkey lettuce wraps are a light yet flavorful lunch option, featuring lean ground turkey and a delicious peanut sauce. It's a low-carb, high-protein meal that's quick to prepare and full of flavor.

Preparation Time: 10 minutes | **Cooking Time**: 10 minutes | **Servings**: 2

Ingredients:

- 200 g ground turkey
- 1 tablespoon (15 ml) olive oil
- 1/2 cup (75 g) bell peppers, sliced
- 1/4 cup (30 g) shredded carrots
- 6 large lettuce leaves (for wrapping)
- 2 tablespoons (30 ml) soy sauce or tamari
- 1 tablespoon (15 g) peanut butter
- 1 tablespoon (15 ml) lime juice
- 1 teaspoon (5 ml) sesame oil
- 1 garlic clove, minced
- Optional: chopped peanuts for garnish

Instructions:

1. Heat the olive oil in a pan over medium heat. Add the ground turkey and cook for 5-6 minutes until browned and fully cooked.
2. Stir in the bell peppers, shredded carrots, and garlic. Cook for another 2-3 minutes.
3. In a small bowl, whisk together the soy sauce, peanut butter, lime juice, and sesame oil until smooth.
4. Spoon the turkey and vegetable mixture into the lettuce leaves.
5. Drizzle with the peanut sauce and garnish with chopped peanuts if desired. Serve immediately.

Nutritional Information (per serving):

Calories: 350 kcal | Protein: 30 g | Carbohydrates: 12 g | Fat: 20 g | Fiber: 5 g

Adapting for Meal Plans:

- For Fat Loss: Use lean ground turkey and reduce the amount of peanut butter to lower fat content.
- For Muscle Building: Add extra turkey or a side of cooked quinoa for additional protein and calories.

Lentil and Chicken Soup

This hearty lentil and chicken soup is a protein-packed, warming lunch option. It combines lean chicken with fiber-rich lentils, making it a filling and nutritious meal that's perfect for any day.

Preparation Time: 10 minutes | **Cooking Time**: 25 minutes | **Servings**: 2

Ingredients:

- 150 g cooked chicken breast, shredded
- 1/2 cup (100 g) dry lentils
- 1 tablespoon (15 ml) olive oil
- 1 small onion, chopped
- 1 carrot, chopped
- 1 celery stalk, chopped
- 2 garlic cloves, minced
- 3 cups (720 ml) chicken broth
- 1/2 teaspoon (2 g) ground cumin
- 1/2 teaspoon (2 g) paprika
- Salt and pepper to taste
- Optional: fresh parsley for garnish

Instructions:

1. Heat the olive oil in a large pot over medium heat. Add the onion, carrot, celery, and garlic, and sauté for 4-5 minutes until softened.
2. Add the lentils, chicken broth, cumin, and paprika to the pot. Bring to a boil, then reduce the heat and simmer for 20-25 minutes until the lentils are tender.
3. Stir in the shredded chicken and season with salt and pepper. Cook for an additional 2-3 minutes until the chicken is heated through.
4. Serve hot, garnished with fresh parsley if desired.

Nutritional Information (per serving):

Calories: 350 kcal | Protein: 30 g | Carbohydrates: 30 g | Fat: 10 g | Fiber: 12 g

Adapting for Meal Plans:

- For Fat Loss: Use less olive oil and a smaller portion of lentils to lower calories and carbohydrates.
- For Muscle Building: Add an extra 50 g of chicken or a side of whole-grain bread for more protein and carbs.

Spaghetti Squash with Ground Beef

This low-carb alternative to traditional spaghetti pairs roasted spaghetti squash with flavorful ground beef, making it a satisfying and nutritious lunch option.

Preparation Time: 10 minutes | **Cooking Time**: 40 minutes | **Servings**: 2

Ingredients:

- 1 medium spaghetti squash
- 200 g ground beef (lean)
- 1 tablespoon (15 ml) olive oil
- 1/2 cup (120 ml) marinara sauce (low-sugar)
- 1/4 cup (30 g) grated Parmesan cheese (optional)
- 1 teaspoon (5 g) garlic powder
- Salt and pepper to taste
- Fresh parsley for garnish (optional)

Instructions:

1. Preheat the oven to 200°C (400°F).
2. Cut the spaghetti squash in half lengthwise and scoop out the seeds. Drizzle the cut sides with olive oil and season with salt and pepper. Place the squash cut side down on a baking sheet and roast for 35-40 minutes until tender.
3. While the squash is roasting, heat a pan over medium heat and cook the ground beef until browned and fully cooked, about 6-8 minutes. Stir in the marinara sauce and garlic powder, and season with salt and pepper.
4. When the spaghetti squash is ready, use a fork to scrape out the flesh, which will form spaghetti-like strands.
5. Serve the ground beef mixture over the spaghetti squash. Top with Parmesan cheese and garnish with fresh parsley if desired.

Nutritional Information (per serving):

Calories: 400 kcal | Protein: 30 g | Carbohydrates: 15 g | Fat: 25 g | Fiber: 6 g

Adapting for Meal Plans:

- For Fat Loss: Use lean ground turkey instead of beef and reduce the portion of cheese to lower fat content.
- For Muscle Building: Add extra ground beef or a side of garlic bread for more protein and calories.

Greek Salad with Grilled Chicken

This Greek-inspired salad combines juicy grilled chicken with fresh vegetables and a tangy dressing, making it a perfect high-protein, low-carb lunch option.

Preparation Time: 10 minutes | **Cooking Time**: 15 minutes | **Servings**: 2

Ingredients:

- 200 g grilled chicken breast, sliced
- 4 cups (120 g) romaine lettuce or mixed greens
- 1/2 cup (75 g) cucumber, diced
- 1/4 cup (60 g) cherry tomatoes, halved
- 1/4 cup (30 g) red onion, thinly sliced
- 1/4 cup (40 g) Kalamata olives, pitted and halved
- 1/4 cup (30 g) feta cheese, crumbled
- 2 tablespoons (30 ml) olive oil
- 1 tablespoon (15 ml) lemon juice
- Salt and pepper to taste
- Optional: fresh oregano for garnish

Instructions:

1. In a large bowl, combine the lettuce, cucumber, cherry tomatoes, red onion, and Kalamata olives.
2. Top the salad with the grilled chicken and crumbled feta cheese.
3. Drizzle with olive oil and lemon juice, and season with salt and pepper.
4. Garnish with fresh oregano if desired, and serve immediately.

Nutritional Information (per serving):

Calories: 420 kcal | Protein: 35 g | Carbohydrates: 10 g | Fat: 28 g | Fiber: 6 g

Adapting for Meal Plans:

- For Fat Loss: Use less olive oil and feta cheese to reduce fat content.
- For Muscle Building: Add an extra 100 g of grilled chicken or serve with a side of whole-grain bread for more protein and carbs.

Baked Cod with Green Beans

This light and nutritious dish combines flaky baked cod with tender green beans for a high-protein, low-carb meal that's easy to prepare and packed with flavor.

Preparation Time: 10 minutes | **Cooking Time**: 15 minutes | **Servings**: 2

Ingredients:

- 200 g cod fillets
- 1 tablespoon (15 ml) olive oil
- 200 g green beans, trimmed
- 1 lemon, sliced
- 2 garlic cloves, minced
- 1/2 teaspoon (2 g) paprika
- Salt and pepper to taste
- Optional: fresh parsley for garnish

Instructions:

1. Preheat the oven to 180°C (350°F).
2. Place the cod fillets on a baking sheet lined with parchment paper. Drizzle with olive oil and season with paprika, salt, pepper, and minced garlic. Top with lemon slices.
3. In a separate baking dish, toss the green beans with olive oil, salt, and pepper.
4. Bake the cod and green beans in the oven for 12-15 minutes, or until the cod is flaky and cooked through.
5. Serve the baked cod with green beans, garnished with fresh parsley if desired.

Nutritional Information (per serving):

Calories: 300 kcal | Protein: 32 g | Carbohydrates: 10 g | Fat: 16 g | Fiber: 4 g

Adapting for Meal Plans:

- For Fat Loss: Use a smaller portion of olive oil and increase the amount of green beans for a filling, lower-calorie option.
- For Muscle Building: Add an extra cod fillet or serve with a side of quinoa for additional protein and carbohydrates.

Eggplant and Ground Turkey Bake

This comforting and flavorful bake pairs tender eggplant with lean ground turkey in a hearty, low-carb meal. It's perfect for a filling lunch that's rich in protein and vegetables.

Preparation Time: 15 minutes | **Cooking Time:** 30 minutes | **Servings:** 2

Ingredients:

- 200 g ground turkey
- 1 medium eggplant, sliced
- 1 tablespoon (15 ml) olive oil
- 1/2 cup (120 ml) marinara sauce (low-sugar)
- 1/4 cup (30 g) grated Parmesan cheese (optional)
- 1/2 teaspoon (2 g) garlic powder
- 1/2 teaspoon (2 g) onion powder
- Salt and pepper to taste
- Fresh basil for garnish (optional)

Instructions:

1. Preheat the oven to 180°C (350°F).
2. In a large pan, heat the olive oil over medium heat. Add the ground turkey and cook until browned, about 6-8 minutes. Season with garlic powder, onion powder, salt, and pepper.
3. While the turkey is cooking, lightly grill the eggplant slices in a separate pan for 2-3 minutes on each side, or until softened.
4. In a baking dish, layer half of the grilled eggplant, then add the cooked turkey and marinara sauce. Top with the remaining eggplant slices.
5. Sprinkle with Parmesan cheese if using, and bake for 20 minutes until the cheese is melted and the dish is bubbly.
6. Garnish with fresh basil if desired and serve warm.

Nutritional Information (per serving):

Calories: 350 kcal | Protein: 30 g | Carbohydrates: 15 g | Fat: 20 g | Fiber: 8 g

Adapting for Meal Plans:

- For Fat Loss: Use less olive oil and skip the Parmesan cheese to reduce fat content.
- For Muscle Building: Add extra ground turkey or a side of whole-grain bread for more protein and carbs.

Pulled Pork Lettuce Wraps

These pulled pork lettuce wraps are a tasty and low-carb lunch option. Tender, slow-cooked pork is served in crisp lettuce leaves, making it a light and flavorful meal that's high in protein.

Preparation Time: 10 minutes | **Cooking Time**: 4-6 hours (in a slow cooker) | **Servings**: 2

Ingredients:

- 200 g pulled pork (cooked in a slow cooker)
- 6 large lettuce leaves (for wrapping)
- 1 tablespoon (15 ml) olive oil
- 1/4 cup (60 g) red cabbage, thinly sliced
- 1/4 cup (60 g) carrot, julienned
- 1 tablespoon (15 ml) apple cider vinegar
- Salt and pepper to taste
- Optional: 1 tablespoon (15 g) BBQ sauce (low-sugar)

Instructions:

1. Prepare the pulled pork by slow cooking the pork in a slow cooker for 4-6 hours with olive oil, salt, pepper, and apple cider vinegar until tender.
2. Once the pork is cooked, shred it using two forks.
3. Assemble the lettuce wraps by placing a portion of the pulled pork in each lettuce leaf.
4. Top with red cabbage, carrot, and a drizzle of low-sugar BBQ sauce if desired.
5. Serve immediately and enjoy.

Nutritional Information (per serving):

Calories: 320 kcal | Protein: 28 g | Carbohydrates: 8 g | Fat: 20 g | Fiber: 4 g

Adapting for Meal Plans:

- For Fat Loss: Use lean pork cuts and reduce the olive oil to lower fat content.
- For Muscle Building: Add extra pulled pork or a side of quinoa for more protein and carbohydrates.

Zucchini Fritters with Smoked Salmon

These crispy zucchini fritters are a delicious low-carb base for savory smoked salmon. Packed with protein and vegetables, this dish is perfect for a light yet satisfying lunch.

Preparation Time: 10 minutes | **Cooking Time:** 10 minutes | **Servings:** 2

Ingredients:

- 2 medium zucchinis, grated
- 1/4 cup (30 g) almond flour
- 2 large eggs
- 1/2 teaspoon (2 g) garlic powder
- 1/2 teaspoon (2 g) onion powder
- Salt and pepper to taste
- 1 tablespoon (15 ml) olive oil (for frying)
- 100 g smoked salmon, sliced
- 1 tablespoon (15 ml) lemon juice
- Optional: fresh dill for garnish

Instructions:

1. Grate the zucchinis and squeeze out excess moisture using a clean kitchen towel.
2. In a bowl, mix the grated zucchini, almond flour, eggs, garlic powder, onion powder, salt, and pepper.
3. Heat the olive oil in a pan over medium heat. Drop spoonfuls of the zucchini mixture into the pan and flatten slightly to form fritters.
4. Fry for 2-3 minutes on each side, until golden brown and crispy. Remove from the pan and drain on paper towels.
5. Serve the fritters topped with smoked salmon and a drizzle of lemon juice. Garnish with fresh dill if desired.

Nutritional Information (per serving):

Calories: 320 kcal | Protein: 22 g | Carbohydrates: 8 g | Fat: 24 g | Fiber: 4 g

Adapting for Meal Plans:

- For Fat Loss: Use less olive oil for frying and reduce the amount of smoked salmon.
- For Muscle Building: Add an extra serving of smoked salmon or top with poached eggs for more protein.

Chicken Tacos with Avocado

These chicken tacos are a perfect low-carb lunch option. Made with lean chicken breast and fresh avocado, they are flavorful, protein-rich, and easy to prepare.

Preparation Time: 10 minutes | **Cooking Time**: 10 minutes | **Servings**: 2

Ingredients:

- 200 g chicken breast, cooked and shredded
- 6 small lettuce leaves (for taco shells)
- 1 avocado, diced
- 1/4 cup (60 g) cherry tomatoes, halved
- 1/4 cup (60 g) red onion, finely diced
- 1 tablespoon (15 ml) lime juice
- 1 tablespoon (15 ml) olive oil
- Salt and pepper to taste
- Optional: fresh cilantro for garnish

Instructions:

1. In a bowl, combine the shredded chicken, lime juice, olive oil, salt, and pepper.
2. Lay out the lettuce leaves and fill each with the shredded chicken mixture.
3. Top with diced avocado, cherry tomatoes, and red onion.
4. Garnish with fresh cilantro if desired, and serve immediately.

Nutritional Information (per serving):

Calories: 350 kcal | Protein: 30 g | Carbohydrates: 12 g | Fat: 22 g | Fiber: 8 g

Adapting for Meal Plans:

- For Fat Loss: Use less avocado and olive oil to lower the fat content.
- For Muscle Building: Add extra chicken or top with shredded cheese for additional protein.

Chapter 4: Nutrient-Dense and Flavorful Dinners

Dinner is the meal where you can fully relax and enjoy a satisfying, balanced plate after a long day. Whether you've spent your time at work, with family, or at the gym, a nutrient-rich dinner provides the fuel your body needs to recover, rebuild, and get ready for the next day. For those following a low-carb, high-protein lifestyle, it's especially important to make dinner a time to nourish your body with lean proteins, healthy fats, and plenty of vegetables.

In this section, we focus on nutritious and flavorful dinner recipes that are simple to prepare yet full of delicious ingredients. From baked salmon to hearty soups, these meals will keep you satisfied without weighing you down.

We'll start with a light yet flavorful dish: Baked Salmon with Asparagus. This combination of tender salmon and crisp asparagus is a classic pairing that's rich in healthy fats and lean protein, perfect for any night of the week.

Baked Salmon with Asparagus

This simple yet flavorful dish combines tender baked salmon with crisp asparagus, making it a perfect high-protein, low-carb dinner option. Rich in healthy fats and omega-3s, it's both nutritious and delicious.

Preparation Time: 10 minutes | **Cooking Time**: 15 minutes | **Servings**: 2

Ingredients:

- 2 salmon fillets (about 200 g each)
- 1 bunch (200 g) asparagus, trimmed
- 1 tablespoon (15 ml) olive oil
- 1 lemon, sliced
- 2 garlic cloves, minced
- Salt and pepper to taste
- Optional: fresh dill for garnish

Instructions:

1. Preheat the oven to 180°C (350°F).
2. Place the salmon fillets on a baking sheet lined with parchment paper. Drizzle with half of the olive oil, season with salt, pepper, and minced garlic, and top with lemon slices.
3. Toss the asparagus in the remaining olive oil, season with salt and pepper, and arrange it around the salmon on the baking sheet.
4. Bake for 12-15 minutes, or until the salmon is cooked through and the asparagus is tender.
5. Garnish with fresh dill if desired, and serve immediately.

Nutritional Information (per serving):

Calories: 400 kcal | Protein: 35 g | Carbohydrates: 8 g | Fat: 25 g | Fiber: 4 g

Adapting for Meal Plans:

- For Fat Loss: Use a smaller portion of salmon and reduce the amount of olive oil.
- For Muscle Building: Add extra salmon or a side of quinoa for more protein and carbohydrates.

Vegetable Soup with Chicken

This hearty vegetable soup with chicken is perfect for a cozy, nutrient-packed dinner. Loaded with lean protein and a variety of vegetables, it's both filling and light, making it ideal for a low-carb, high-protein lifestyle.

Preparation Time: 10 minutes | **Cooking Time**: 20 minutes | **Servings**: 2

Ingredients:

- 200 g cooked chicken breast, shredded
- 1 tablespoon (15 ml) olive oil
- 1 small onion, chopped
- 1 carrot, chopped
- 1 celery stalk, chopped
- 2 garlic cloves, minced
- 3 cups (720 ml) chicken broth
- 1 cup (150 g) zucchini, chopped
- 1/2 cup (75 g) bell peppers, chopped
- 1/2 teaspoon (2 g) dried thyme
- Salt and pepper to taste
- Optional: fresh parsley for garnish

Instructions:

1. Heat the olive oil in a large pot over medium heat. Add the onion, carrot, celery, and garlic, and sauté for 5 minutes until softened.
2. Add the chicken broth, zucchini, bell peppers, thyme, salt, and pepper. Bring to a boil, then reduce the heat and simmer for 10-15 minutes, until the vegetables are tender.
3. Stir in the shredded chicken and cook for an additional 2-3 minutes until heated through.
4. Serve hot, garnished with fresh parsley if desired.

Nutritional Information (per serving):

Calories: 300 kcal | Protein: 30 g | Carbohydrates: 12 g | Fat: 15 g | Fiber: 5 g

Adapting for Meal Plans:

- For Fat Loss: Use less olive oil and increase the amount of vegetables for a lighter, lower-calorie option.
- For Muscle Building: Add extra chicken or serve with a side of whole-grain bread for additional protein and carbohydrates.

Grilled Steak with Sweet Potatoes

This grilled steak with sweet potatoes is a balanced, protein-rich dinner that's perfect for satisfying hunger while keeping your carb intake moderate. The sweet potatoes provide a good source of complex carbohydrates, while the steak adds lean protein and essential nutrients.

Preparation Time: 10 minutes | **Cooking Time**: 20 minutes | **Servings**: 2

Ingredients:

- 200 g lean steak (sirloin or flank)
- 2 small sweet potatoes, cut into wedges
- 1 tablespoon (15 ml) olive oil
- 1 teaspoon (5 g) garlic powder
- 1 teaspoon (5 g) paprika
- Salt and pepper to taste
- Optional: fresh rosemary for garnish

Instructions:

1. Preheat the oven to 200°C (400°F). Toss the sweet potato wedges with half of the olive oil, garlic powder, paprika, salt, and pepper. Spread them on a baking sheet and roast for 20 minutes, turning halfway through.
2. Meanwhile, heat the remaining olive oil in a grill pan over medium-high heat. Season the steak with salt and pepper, and grill for 4-5 minutes on each side, or until cooked to your desired doneness.
3. Let the steak rest for a few minutes before slicing.
4. Serve the grilled steak with the roasted sweet potatoes, garnished with fresh rosemary if desired.

Nutritional Information (per serving):

Calories: 450 kcal | Protein: 30 g | Carbohydrates: 30 g | Fat: 22 g | Fiber: 5 g

Adapting for Meal Plans:

- For Fat Loss: Use a leaner cut of steak and reduce the amount of sweet potatoes to lower carbohydrates.
- For Muscle Building: Increase the portion of steak or add extra sweet potatoes for more protein and carbohydrates.

Chicken Curry with Brown Rice

This flavorful chicken curry served with brown rice is a nutrient-dense, high-protein meal that combines lean chicken with the warming spices of curry. It's a satisfying and balanced dinner option that's rich in protein and complex carbohydrates.

Preparation Time: 10 minutes | **Cooking Time:** 25 minutes | **Servings:** 2

Ingredients:

- 200 g chicken breast, cut into cubes
- 1 tablespoon (15 ml) coconut oil
- 1 small onion, chopped
- 1 garlic clove, minced
- 1 tablespoon (15 g) curry powder
- 1/2 teaspoon (2 g) turmeric
- 1/2 cup (120 ml) coconut milk (light)
- 1/2 cup (90 g) brown rice (uncooked)
- 1 cup (150 g) broccoli florets
- Salt and pepper to taste
- Optional: fresh cilantro for garnish

Instructions:

1. Cook the brown rice according to the package instructions.
2. In a large pan, heat the coconut oil over medium heat. Add the onion and garlic, and sauté for 3-4 minutes until softened.
3. Stir in the curry powder and turmeric, and cook for another minute until fragrant.
4. Add the chicken cubes and cook for 6-7 minutes until browned and fully cooked.
5. Stir in the coconut milk and broccoli, and simmer for 5 minutes until the broccoli is tender. Season with salt and pepper.
6. Serve the chicken curry over the cooked brown rice, garnished with fresh cilantro if desired.

Nutritional Information (per serving):

Calories: 450 kcal | Protein: 35 g | Carbohydrates: 35 g | Fat: 18 g | Fiber: 6 g

Adapting for Meal Plans:

- For Fat Loss: Use less coconut milk and reduce the portion of brown rice to lower fat and carbohydrate content.
- For Muscle Building: Increase the portion of chicken or brown rice for more protein and complex carbohydrates.

Lemon Garlic Shrimp with Cauliflower Rice

This light and zesty lemon garlic shrimp served over cauliflower rice is a perfect low-carb, high-protein dinner option. It's quick to prepare, full of flavor, and rich in essential nutrients, making it ideal for a healthy, balanced meal.

Preparation Time: 10 minutes | **Cooking Time**: 10 minutes | **Servings**: 2

Ingredients:

- 200 g shrimp, peeled and deveined
- 2 cups (200 g) cauliflower rice
- 1 tablespoon (15 ml) olive oil
- 2 garlic cloves, minced
- 1 lemon, juiced
- 1/4 teaspoon (1 g) red pepper flakes (optional)
- Salt and pepper to taste
- Optional: fresh parsley for garnish

Instructions:

1. Heat half of the olive oil in a pan over medium heat. Add the shrimp, garlic, and red pepper flakes, and cook for 2-3 minutes on each side until the shrimp are pink and fully cooked. Drizzle with lemon juice and season with salt and pepper. Remove from heat.
2. In a separate pan, heat the remaining olive oil and sauté the cauliflower rice for 4-5 minutes until tender. Season with salt and pepper.
3. Serve the shrimp over the cauliflower rice, garnished with fresh parsley if desired.

Nutritional Information (per serving):

Calories: 280 kcal | Protein: 30 g | Carbohydrates: 8 g | Fat: 15 g | Fiber: 4 g

Adapting for Meal Plans:

- For Fat Loss: Use less olive oil and increase the portion of cauliflower rice to keep the meal light.
- For Muscle Building: Add extra shrimp or serve with a side of quinoa for more protein and carbohydrates.

Baked Chicken Thighs with Brussels Sprouts

This baked chicken thighs and Brussels sprouts dish is rich in protein and healthy fats, offering a satisfying and nutritious dinner option. The crispy chicken pairs perfectly with roasted Brussels sprouts, making it a simple yet flavorful meal.

Preparation Time: 10 minutes | **Cooking Time**: 30 minutes | **Servings**: 2

Ingredients:

- 4 chicken thighs (about 400 g)
- 200 g Brussels sprouts, halved
- 1 tablespoon (15 ml) olive oil
- 1 teaspoon (5 g) garlic powder
- 1 teaspoon (5 g) paprika
- Salt and pepper to taste
- Optional: lemon wedges for serving

Instructions:

1. Preheat the oven to 200°C (400°F).
2. Place the chicken thighs on a baking sheet. Drizzle with half the olive oil and season with garlic powder, paprika, salt, and pepper.
3. Toss the Brussels sprouts in the remaining olive oil and season with salt and pepper. Arrange them around the chicken thighs on the baking sheet.
4. Bake for 25-30 minutes, or until the chicken thighs are fully cooked and the skin is crispy, and the Brussels sprouts are tender and golden.
5. Serve with lemon wedges for added flavor if desired.

Nutritional Information (per serving):

Calories: 450 kcal | Protein: 35 g | Carbohydrates: 10 g | Fat: 30 g | Fiber: 5 g

Adapting for Meal Plans:

- For Fat Loss: Use skinless chicken thighs and reduce the amount of olive oil for lower fat content.
- For Muscle Building: Add an extra chicken thigh or serve with a side of quinoa for more protein and carbohydrates.

Lamb Chops with Spinach and Feta

This flavorful dish pairs tender lamb chops with a rich spinach and feta side, making it a nutrient-dense, high-protein dinner option. The combination of savory lamb with the creamy feta and sautéed spinach creates a perfect balance of flavors.

Preparation Time: 10 minutes | **Cooking Time**: 15 minutes | **Servings**: 2

Ingredients:

- 4 lamb chops (about 300 g)
- 1 tablespoon (15 ml) olive oil
- 2 garlic cloves, minced
- 200 g fresh spinach
- 1/4 cup (30 g) crumbled feta cheese
- 1 teaspoon (5 g) dried oregano
- Salt and pepper to taste
- Optional: lemon wedges for serving

Instructions:

1. Heat half of the olive oil in a pan over medium-high heat. Season the lamb chops with salt, pepper, and oregano, and cook for 3-4 minutes on each side until browned and cooked to your preferred doneness. Remove from the pan and let rest.
2. In the same pan, add the remaining olive oil and minced garlic. Sauté for 1 minute, then add the spinach and cook for 2-3 minutes until wilted.
3. Stir in the crumbled feta cheese and season with salt and pepper.
4. Serve the lamb chops alongside the spinach and feta mixture, with lemon wedges for added flavor if desired.

Nutritional Information (per serving):

Calories: 480 kcal | Protein: 35 g | Carbohydrates: 8 g | Fat: 35 g | Fiber: 3 g

Adapting for Meal Plans:

- For Fat Loss: Use a smaller portion of lamb and reduce the amount of feta cheese for a lighter option.
- For Muscle Building: Add an extra lamb chop or serve with a side of whole-grain bread for more protein and carbohydrates.

Grilled Mackerel with Roasted Vegetables

This grilled mackerel dish is rich in omega-3 fatty acids and protein, served with a side of roasted vegetables for a nutrient-dense and flavorful dinner. The combination of crispy mackerel and caramelized vegetables makes this meal both healthy and satisfying.

Preparation Time: 10 minutes | **Cooking Time:** 20 minutes | **Servings:** 2

Ingredients:

- 2 whole mackerel fillets (about 300 g)
- 1 tablespoon (15 ml) olive oil
- 1 zucchini, chopped
- 1 red bell pepper, sliced
- 1 small red onion, sliced
- 1 teaspoon (5 g) dried thyme
- Salt and pepper to taste
- Optional: lemon wedges for serving

Instructions:

1. Preheat the oven to 200°C (400°F). Toss the zucchini, red bell pepper, and onion with half of the olive oil, thyme, salt, and pepper. Spread the vegetables on a baking sheet and roast for 20 minutes, turning halfway through.
2. While the vegetables are roasting, heat the remaining olive oil in a grill pan over medium-high heat. Season the mackerel fillets with salt and pepper, and grill for 3-4 minutes on each side, until the skin is crispy and the fish is cooked through.
3. Serve the grilled mackerel alongside the roasted vegetables, with lemon wedges for added flavor if desired.

Nutritional Information (per serving):

Calories: 450 kcal | Protein: 35 g | Carbohydrates: 12 g | Fat: 28 g | Fiber: 6 g

Adapting for Meal Plans:

- For Fat Loss: Use a smaller portion of mackerel and reduce the olive oil for a lighter option.
- For Muscle Building: Add extra mackerel or serve with a side of quinoa for more protein and carbohydrates.

Seared Tuna Steak with Broccoli

This seared tuna steak with broccoli is a light yet filling meal, packed with lean protein and healthy fats. It's quick to prepare and perfect for a nutritious dinner that's low in carbs but high in flavor.

Preparation Time: 5 minutes | **Cooking Time**: 10 minutes | **Servings**: 2

Ingredients:

- 2 tuna steaks (about 200 g each)
- 1 tablespoon (15 ml) olive oil
- 1 tablespoon (15 ml) soy sauce or tamari
- 1 teaspoon (5 ml) sesame oil
- 1 teaspoon (5 g) sesame seeds (optional)
- 2 cups (150 g) broccoli florets
- Salt and pepper to taste
- Optional: fresh ginger for garnish

Instructions:

1. Heat half of the olive oil in a pan over medium-high heat. Season the tuna steaks with salt and pepper. Sear the tuna for 2-3 minutes on each side, depending on your preferred level of doneness. Remove from the pan and let rest.
2. In the same pan, add the remaining olive oil and sauté the broccoli florets for 4-5 minutes until tender. Drizzle with soy sauce or tamari and sesame oil, and sprinkle with sesame seeds if desired.
3. Serve the seared tuna steaks with the sautéed broccoli, garnished with fresh ginger if desired.

Nutritional Information (per serving):

Calories: 350 kcal | Protein: 40 g | Carbohydrates: 8 g | Fat: 18 g | Fiber: 4 g

Adapting for Meal Plans:

- For Fat Loss: Use less sesame oil and opt for a smaller portion of tuna for a lighter option.
- For Muscle Building: Add extra tuna or serve with a side of brown rice for more protein and carbohydrates.

Turkey Meatloaf with Mashed Cauliflower

This lean turkey meatloaf paired with creamy mashed cauliflower is a comforting, high-protein meal. It's low in carbs and packed with flavor, making it a perfect healthy dinner option.

Preparation Time: 15 minutes | **Cooking Time**: 40 minutes | **Servings**: 2

Ingredients:

- 200 g ground turkey
- 1/4 cup (30 g) almond flour (or breadcrumbs)
- 1 egg
- 1 small onion, finely diced
- 1 garlic clove, minced
- 1 tablespoon (15 ml) tomato paste
- 1 teaspoon (5 g) dried oregano
- Salt and pepper to taste
- 1 medium cauliflower head, chopped
- 1 tablespoon (15 ml) olive oil (for mashed cauliflower)
- 1/4 cup (60 ml) milk or almond milk (for mashed cauliflower)
- Optional: fresh parsley for garnish

Instructions:

1. Preheat the oven to 180°C (350°F).
2. In a bowl, combine the ground turkey, almond flour, egg, onion, garlic, tomato paste, oregano, salt, and pepper. Mix well and shape the mixture into a small loaf.
3. Place the turkey loaf in a baking dish and bake for 30-35 minutes until cooked through.
4. While the meatloaf is baking, steam the cauliflower until tender, about 10 minutes. Drain and transfer to a blender or food processor.
5. Add the olive oil and milk to the cauliflower, and blend until smooth and creamy. Season with salt and pepper to taste.
6. Serve the turkey meatloaf with mashed cauliflower, garnished with fresh parsley if desired.

Nutritional Information (per serving):

Calories: 400 kcal | Protein: 35 g | Carbohydrates: 15 g | Fat: 20 g | Fiber: 7 g

Adapting for Meal Plans:

- For Fat Loss: Use less olive oil and almond flour for a lighter version of the dish.
- For Muscle Building: Add extra turkey or a side of quinoa for more protein and carbohydrates.

Eggplant Parmesan with Ground Beef

This Eggplant Parmesan with ground beef is a delicious low-carb take on the classic Italian dish. It's layered with tender eggplant, savory ground beef, and a rich tomato sauce, making it a filling, high-protein dinner option.

Preparation Time: 15 minutes | **Cooking Time**: 30 minutes | **Servings**: 2

Ingredients:

- 1 medium eggplant, sliced
- 200 g ground beef (lean)
- 1 cup (240 ml) marinara sauce (low-sugar)
- 1/4 cup (30 g) grated Parmesan cheese
- 1/2 cup (60 g) shredded mozzarella cheese
- 1 tablespoon (15 ml) olive oil
- 1 teaspoon (5 g) garlic powder
- Salt and pepper to taste
- Optional: fresh basil for garnish

Instructions:

1. Preheat the oven to 180°C (350°F).
2. Lightly grill or bake the eggplant slices for 5-7 minutes, until they are softened.
3. In a pan, heat the olive oil over medium heat. Add the ground beef and cook until browned, about 6-8 minutes. Season with garlic powder, salt, and pepper.
4. In a baking dish, layer half of the eggplant slices, followed by half of the ground beef and half of the marinara sauce.
5. Repeat the layers and top with mozzarella and Parmesan cheese.
6. Bake for 20 minutes, or until the cheese is melted and bubbly.
7. Garnish with fresh basil and serve hot.

Nutritional Information (per serving):

Calories: 450 kcal | Protein: 35 g | Carbohydrates: 15 g | Fat: 30 g | Fiber: 7 g

Adapting for Meal Plans:

- For Fat Loss: Use less cheese and lean ground turkey instead of beef to reduce fat content.
- For Muscle Building: Add extra ground beef or serve with a side of whole-grain bread for more protein and carbohydrates.

Roasted Duck Breast with Mushrooms

This roasted duck breast paired with sautéed mushrooms is a rich and flavorful dinner option, perfect for a special occasion or a high-protein, low-carb meal. Duck is a great source of healthy fats and protein, while the mushrooms add an earthy depth to the dish.

Preparation Time: 10 minutes | **Cooking Time:** 25 minutes | **Servings:** 2

Ingredients:

- 2 duck breasts (about 300 g)
- 1 tablespoon (15 ml) olive oil
- 200 g mushrooms, sliced
- 1 garlic clove, minced
- 1 tablespoon (15 ml) balsamic vinegar
- Salt and pepper to taste
- Optional: fresh thyme for garnish

Instructions:

1. Preheat the oven to 200°C (400°F).
2. Score the skin of the duck breasts and season with salt and pepper.
3. Heat a pan over medium heat and place the duck breasts skin-side down. Cook for 6-8 minutes, or until the skin is crispy and golden. Turn the duck breasts over and sear for another 2 minutes.
4. Transfer the duck breasts to a baking sheet and roast in the oven for 8-10 minutes, or until the internal temperature reaches 65°C (150°F).
5. In the same pan, add the olive oil and sauté the mushrooms with the garlic for 3-4 minutes until tender. Deglaze the pan with balsamic vinegar, and season with salt and pepper.
6. Let the duck breasts rest for a few minutes before slicing. Serve with the sautéed mushrooms and garnish with fresh thyme if desired.

Nutritional Information (per serving):

Calories: 500 kcal | Protein: 35 g | Carbohydrates: 10 g | Fat: 35 g | Fiber: 3 g

Adapting for Meal Plans:

- For Fat Loss: Use skinless duck breasts and reduce the amount of olive oil for a lighter version of the dish.
- For Muscle Building: Add an extra duck breast or serve with a side of roasted sweet potatoes for more protein and carbohydrates.

Pork Tenderloin with Cabbage

This pork tenderloin with sautéed cabbage is a simple yet hearty dish that's rich in protein and fiber. It's a perfect low-carb, high-protein dinner option that's flavorful and easy to prepare.

Preparation Time: 10 minutes | **Cooking Time**: 20 minutes | **Servings**: 2

Ingredients:

- 200 g pork tenderloin
- 1 tablespoon (15 ml) olive oil
- 1/2 head of cabbage, thinly sliced
- 1 small onion, chopped
- 1 garlic clove, minced
- 1 tablespoon (15 ml) apple cider vinegar
- Salt and pepper to taste
- Optional: fresh parsley for garnish

Instructions:

1. Heat half of the olive oil in a pan over medium-high heat. Season the pork tenderloin with salt and pepper, and sear for 2-3 minutes on each side until browned. Transfer the pork to a baking dish and roast in a preheated oven at 180°C (350°F) for 15 minutes, or until the internal temperature reaches 65°C (150°F).
2. While the pork is roasting, heat the remaining olive oil in the same pan and sauté the onion and garlic for 2-3 minutes until softened.
3. Add the cabbage to the pan and cook for 5-7 minutes, stirring occasionally, until tender. Stir in the apple cider vinegar and season with salt and pepper.
4. Let the pork rest for a few minutes before slicing. Serve with the sautéed cabbage and garnish with fresh parsley if desired.

Nutritional Information (per serving):

Calories: 350 kcal | Protein: 30 g | Carbohydrates: 12 g | Fat: 20 g | Fiber: 5 g

Adapting for Meal Plans:

- For Fat Loss: Use less olive oil and a smaller portion of pork for a lighter version.
- For Muscle Building: Add extra pork tenderloin or serve with a side of roasted potatoes for more protein and carbohydrates.

Spaghetti Squash with Pesto and Chicken

This low-carb alternative to pasta combines roasted spaghetti squash with a flavorful pesto sauce and lean chicken, making it a satisfying and nutritious dinner option that's packed with protein and healthy fats.

Preparation Time: 10 minutes | **Cooking Time**: 40 minutes | **Servings**: 2

Ingredients:

- 1 medium spaghetti squash
- 200 g cooked chicken breast, shredded
- 1/4 cup (60 ml) basil pesto (homemade or store-bought)
- 1 tablespoon (15 ml) olive oil
- Salt and pepper to taste
- Optional: grated Parmesan cheese for topping

Instructions:

1. Preheat the oven to 200°C (400°F).
2. Cut the spaghetti squash in half lengthwise and remove the seeds. Drizzle the cut sides with olive oil and season with salt and pepper. Place the squash cut side down on a baking sheet and roast for 35-40 minutes until tender.
3. While the squash is roasting, prepare the chicken by shredding the cooked breast and mixing it with the pesto.
4. When the spaghetti squash is done, use a fork to scrape out the strands, which will resemble spaghetti.
5. Toss the spaghetti squash with the pesto chicken mixture and serve hot, topped with Parmesan cheese if desired.

Nutritional Information (per serving):

Calories: 400 kcal | Protein: 30 g | Carbohydrates: 12 g | Fat: 26 g | Fiber: 5 g

Adapting for Meal Plans:

- For Fat Loss: Use less olive oil and pesto to reduce the fat content.
- For Muscle Building: Add extra chicken or top with more Parmesan cheese for additional protein and calories.

Chicken Fajitas with Peppers and Onions

These chicken fajitas are packed with lean protein and colorful vegetables, making them a flavorful and healthy dinner option. Serve with low-carb tortillas or lettuce wraps for a low-carb, high-protein meal.

Preparation Time: 10 minutes | **Cooking Time**: 15 minutes | **Servings**: 2

Ingredients:

- 200 g chicken breast, sliced into strips
- 1 tablespoon (15 ml) olive oil
- 1 red bell pepper, sliced
- 1 green bell pepper, sliced
- 1 small onion, sliced
- 1 teaspoon (5 g) ground cumin
- 1 teaspoon (5 g) smoked paprika
- 1/2 teaspoon (2 g) garlic powder
- Salt and pepper to taste
- Optional: low-carb tortillas or lettuce wraps for serving
- Optional: fresh cilantro and lime wedges for garnish

Instructions:

1. Heat the olive oil in a large pan over medium-high heat. Add the sliced chicken breast and cook for 5-6 minutes until golden and cooked through.
2. Add the sliced peppers, onions, cumin, paprika, garlic powder, salt, and pepper. Cook for an additional 5-7 minutes until the vegetables are tender.
3. Serve the chicken and vegetable mixture with low-carb tortillas or lettuce wraps. Garnish with fresh cilantro and lime wedges if desired.

Nutritional Information (per serving):

Calories: 350 kcal | Protein: 30 g | Carbohydrates: 12 g | Fat: 18 g | Fiber: 4 g

Adapting for Meal Plans:

- For Fat Loss: Use less olive oil and serve with lettuce wraps instead of tortillas to reduce calories and fat.
- For Muscle Building: Add extra chicken or serve with a side of rice or quinoa for additional protein and carbohydrates.

Slow-Cooked Beef Stew

This hearty slow-cooked beef stew is packed with lean beef and vegetables, making it a perfect comfort food for dinner. It's rich in protein and ideal for a low-carb, high-protein lifestyle.

Preparation Time: 15 minutes | **Cooking Time**: 6-8 hours (in a slow cooker) | **Servings**: 4

Ingredients:

- 400 g lean beef stew meat, cubed
- 2 tablespoons (30 ml) olive oil
- 1 onion, chopped
- 2 garlic cloves, minced
- 2 carrots, chopped
- 1 celery stalk, chopped
- 1 zucchini, chopped
- 3 cups (720 ml) beef broth
- 1 tablespoon (15 ml) tomato paste
- 1 teaspoon (5 g) dried thyme
- 1 teaspoon (5 g) paprika
- Salt and pepper to taste
- Optional: fresh parsley for garnish

Instructions:

1. In a large pan, heat the olive oil over medium heat. Add the beef and sear for 4-5 minutes until browned on all sides. Remove and transfer to a slow cooker.
2. In the same pan, sauté the onion, garlic, carrots, and celery for 3-4 minutes until softened. Add to the slow cooker.
3. Add the zucchini, beef broth, tomato paste, thyme, paprika, salt, and pepper to the slow cooker. Stir to combine.
4. Cover and cook on low for 6-8 hours, or until the beef is tender and the flavors are well combined.
5. Serve hot, garnished with fresh parsley if desired.

Nutritional Information (per serving):

Calories: 380 kcal | Protein: 30 g | Carbohydrates: 12 g | Fat: 22 g | Fiber: 4 g

Adapting for Meal Plans:

- For Fat Loss: Use less olive oil and reduce the portion of beef for a lighter option.
- For Muscle Building: Add extra beef or serve with a side of quinoa for more protein and carbohydrates.

Grilled Pork Chops with Asparagus

This simple yet delicious grilled pork chop recipe pairs perfectly with tender asparagus. It's a high-protein, low-carb dinner that's easy to prepare and full of flavor.

Preparation Time: 10 minutes | **Cooking Time**: 15 minutes | **Servings**: 2

Ingredients:

- 2 pork chops (about 200 g each)
- 1 bunch (200 g) asparagus, trimmed
- 1 tablespoon (15 ml) olive oil
- 1 teaspoon (5 g) garlic powder
- 1 teaspoon (5 g) paprika
- Salt and pepper to taste
- Optional: lemon wedges for serving

Instructions:

1. Preheat the grill to medium-high heat.
2. Rub the pork chops with olive oil, garlic powder, paprika, salt, and pepper.
3. Grill the pork chops for 5-6 minutes on each side until cooked through. Remove from the grill and let rest.
4. While the pork chops are resting, toss the asparagus with olive oil, salt, and pepper, and grill for 3-4 minutes until tender.
5. Serve the pork chops with grilled asparagus, and garnish with lemon wedges if desired.

Nutritional Information (per serving):

Calories: 400 kcal | Protein: 35 g | Carbohydrates: 10 g | Fat: 25 g | Fiber: 5 g

Adapting for Meal Plans:

- For Fat Loss: Use leaner pork chops and reduce the olive oil to lower fat content.
- For Muscle Building: Add extra pork chops or serve with a side of quinoa for more protein and carbohydrates.

Shrimp Scampi with Zoodles

This shrimp scampi recipe is a low-carb twist on the classic dish, using zucchini noodles instead of pasta. It's light, flavorful, and packed with protein from the shrimp.

Preparation Time: 10 minutes | **Cooking Time**: 10 minutes | **Servings**: 2

Ingredients:

- 200 g shrimp, peeled and deveined
- 2 medium zucchinis, spiralized into noodles
- 1 tablespoon (15 ml) olive oil
- 2 garlic cloves, minced
- 1 lemon, juiced
- 1/4 teaspoon (1 g) red pepper flakes (optional)
- Salt and pepper to taste
- Optional: fresh parsley for garnish

Instructions:

1. Heat the olive oil in a large pan over medium heat. Add the garlic and sauté for 1-2 minutes until fragrant.
2. Add the shrimp and cook for 2-3 minutes on each side until pink and cooked through.
3. Stir in the lemon juice, red pepper flakes, salt, and pepper.
4. Add the zucchini noodles and toss to coat. Cook for an additional 2-3 minutes until the zoodles are tender.
5. Serve hot, garnished with fresh parsley if desired.

Nutritional Information (per serving):

Calories: 300 kcal | Protein: 25 g | Carbohydrates: 10 g | Fat: 18 g | Fiber: 5 g

Adapting for Meal Plans:

- For Fat Loss: Use less olive oil and increase the portion of zucchini noodles for a lighter meal.
- For Muscle Building: Add extra shrimp or serve with a side of quinoa for more protein and carbohydrates.

Baked Tilapia with Spinach

This baked tilapia with sautéed spinach is a light and nutritious meal that's rich in protein and low in carbs. It's simple to make and perfect for a healthy dinner.

Preparation Time: 10 minutes | **Cooking Time**: 15 minutes | **Servings**: 2

Ingredients:

- 2 tilapia fillets (about 150 g each)
- 1 tablespoon (15 ml) olive oil
- 200 g fresh spinach
- 1 garlic clove, minced
- 1 lemon, sliced
- Salt and pepper to taste
- Optional: fresh parsley for garnish

Instructions:

1. Preheat the oven to 180°C (350°F).
2. Place the tilapia fillets on a baking sheet, drizzle with olive oil, and season with salt, pepper, and garlic. Top with lemon slices.
3. Bake for 12-15 minutes, or until the tilapia is cooked through and flaky.
4. While the fish is baking, sauté the spinach in a pan over medium heat until wilted, about 3-4 minutes.
5. Serve the baked tilapia with sautéed spinach, garnished with fresh parsley if desired.

Nutritional Information (per serving):

Calories: 300 kcal | Protein: 30 g | Carbohydrates: 8 g | Fat: 18 g | Fiber: 4 g

Adapting for Meal Plans:

- For Fat Loss: Use less olive oil and increase the portion of spinach for a lighter meal.
- For Muscle Building: Add extra tilapia or serve with a side of quinoa for more protein and carbohydrates.

Chicken Alfredo with Zucchini Noodles

This low-carb chicken Alfredo uses zucchini noodles instead of pasta, making it a lighter version of the classic dish while still rich in protein and flavor.

Preparation Time: 10 minutes | **Cooking Time**: 15 minutes | **Servings**: 2

Ingredients:

- 200 g chicken breast, sliced
- 2 medium zucchinis, spiralized into noodles
- 1 tablespoon (15 ml) olive oil
- 1/2 cup (120 ml) heavy cream
- 1/4 cup (30 g) grated Parmesan cheese
- 1 garlic clove, minced
- Salt and pepper to taste
- Optional: fresh parsley for garnish

Instructions:

1. Heat the olive oil in a large pan over medium heat. Add the chicken slices and cook for 5-6 minutes until golden and cooked through. Remove from the pan and set aside.
2. In the same pan, add the garlic and sauté for 1-2 minutes. Stir in the heavy cream and Parmesan cheese, and cook for 2-3 minutes until the sauce thickens.
3. Add the zucchini noodles to the pan and toss to coat. Cook for an additional 2-3 minutes until the zoodles are tender.
4. Return the chicken to the pan, mix well, and season with salt and pepper.
5. Serve hot, garnished with fresh parsley if desired.

Nutritional Information (per serving):

Calories: 450 kcal | Protein: 35 g | Carbohydrates: 10 g | Fat: 30 g | Fiber: 5 g

Adapting for Meal Plans:

- For Fat Loss: Use light cream and reduce the amount of Parmesan cheese for a lighter meal.
- For Muscle Building: Add extra chicken or serve with a side of brown rice for more protein and carbohydrates.

Chapter 5: Healthy and Easy-to-Make Snacks

When it comes to staying on track with your health goals, having the right snacks at hand is crucial. Whether you're managing hunger between meals, refueling after a workout, or just looking for a quick, nutritious bite, high-protein, low-carb snacks are your best ally. The right snack can keep you energized and satisfied, helping you avoid unhealthy choices.

In this section, you'll find a variety of easy-to-make, protein-packed snacks that fit perfectly into your low-carb, high-protein lifestyle. From savory bites to satisfying sweet treats, these snacks are designed to support your fitness goals while keeping things simple and delicious.

Let's begin with a classic, easy-to-prepare option: Hummus and Celery Sticks—a light and crunchy snack perfect for when you need a quick energy boost.

Hummus and Celery Sticks

This simple snack pairs creamy hummus with crisp celery sticks for a light, protein-rich, and low-carb option that's perfect for a quick energy boost.

Preparation Time: 5 minutes | **Servings**: 2

Ingredients:

- 1/2 cup (120 g) hummus
- 4-6 celery sticks, cut into halves
- Optional: sprinkle of paprika or olive oil on hummus for garnish

Instructions:

1. Arrange the celery sticks on a plate.
2. Serve with a small bowl of hummus, garnished with paprika or a drizzle of olive oil if desired.
3. Enjoy this simple and healthy snack!

Nutritional Information (per serving):

Calories: 150 kcal | Protein: 5 g | Carbohydrates: 10 g | Fat: 10 g | Fiber: 4 g

Adapting for Meal Plans:

- For Fat Loss: Use a lower-fat hummus to reduce calorie intake.
- For Muscle Building: Add a side of boiled eggs or turkey slices for more protein.

Hard-Boiled Eggs with Sunflower Seeds

This high-protein snack combines the simplicity of hard-boiled eggs with a crunchy sunflower seed topping, making it a quick and satisfying option. It's perfect for keeping you full between meals and supports muscle recovery.

Preparation Time: 10 minutes | **Servings**: 2

Ingredients:

- 4 large eggs
- 2 tablespoons (30 g) sunflower seeds
- Salt and pepper to taste
- Optional: a sprinkle of paprika or chili flakes for extra flavor

Instructions:

1. Place the eggs in a saucepan and cover with water. Bring to a boil, then reduce the heat and simmer for 8-10 minutes until fully cooked.
2. Drain and peel the eggs.
3. Serve the eggs sliced or whole, topped with sunflower seeds. Season with salt, pepper, and optional paprika or chili flakes for added flavor.

Nutritional Information (per serving):

Calories: 250 kcal | Protein: 18 g | Carbohydrates: 2 g | Fat: 20 g | Fiber: 2 g

Adapting for Meal Plans:

- For Fat Loss: Use fewer sunflower seeds or replace them with a small amount of ground flaxseed for a lighter option.
- For Muscle Building: Add an extra egg or pair the snack with a small piece of avocado for more protein and healthy fats.

Homemade Protein Bars

These homemade protein bars are a nutritious, high-protein snack that's perfect for a post-workout boost or a quick bite on the go. Made with simple ingredients, they're customizable and much healthier than store-bought options.

Preparation Time: 10 minutes | **Chilling Time:** 1 hour | **Servings:** 4 bars

Ingredients:

- 1/2 cup (120 g) vanilla protein powder
- 1/2 cup (120 g) peanut butter (or almond butter)
- 1/4 cup (60 ml) almond milk (or any milk of your choice)
- 2 tablespoons (30 g) chia seeds or flaxseeds
- 1 tablespoon (15 g) honey (optional for sweetness)
- Optional: dark chocolate chips for topping

Instructions:

1. In a large bowl, mix the protein powder, peanut butter, almond milk, chia seeds, and honey (if using) until well combined. The mixture should be thick but smooth.
2. Press the mixture into a small pan or baking dish lined with parchment paper.
3. Optionally, sprinkle the top with dark chocolate chips and press them gently into the mixture.
4. Place the pan in the fridge to chill for at least 1 hour.
5. Once firm, cut into bars and enjoy. Store in the fridge for up to a week.

Nutritional Information (per bar):

Calories: 220 kcal | Protein: 15 g | Carbohydrates: 10 g | Fat: 14 g | Fiber: 4 g

Adapting for Meal Plans:

- For Fat Loss: Use powdered peanut butter and reduce the amount of honey to lower calories and fat content.
- For Muscle Building: Add extra protein powder or use whole milk for more protein and calories.

Peanut Butter Protein Shake

This creamy peanut butter protein shake is a quick and delicious way to fuel your body with protein and healthy fats. It's perfect for a post-workout recovery or a filling snack between meals.

Preparation Time: 5 minutes | **Servings**: 1

Ingredients:

- 1 scoop (30 g) vanilla protein powder
- 1 tablespoon (15 g) peanut butter
- 1 cup (240 ml) unsweetened almond milk (or any milk of your choice)
- 1/2 banana (for added creaminess and sweetness)
- 1/4 teaspoon (1 g) cinnamon (optional)
- Ice cubes (optional for thickness)

Instructions:

1. Place all the ingredients in a blender.
2. Blend until smooth and creamy. Add ice cubes if you prefer a thicker shake.
3. Pour into a glass and enjoy immediately.

Nutritional Information (per serving):

Calories: 300 kcal | Protein: 25 g | Carbohydrates: 15 g | Fat: 15 g | Fiber: 4 g

Adapting for Meal Plans:

- For Fat Loss: Use powdered peanut butter and reduce the portion of banana to lower the calorie content.
- For Muscle Building: Add an extra scoop of protein powder or a spoonful of Greek yogurt for more protein and calories.

Greek Yogurt with Flax Seeds

This simple snack combines creamy Greek yogurt with the added fiber and healthy fats from flax seeds. It's a quick, high-protein option that supports digestion and overall wellness.

Preparation Time: 5 minutes | **Servings**: 1

Ingredients:

- 1/2 cup (120 g) plain Greek yogurt (unsweetened)
- 1 tablespoon (15 g) ground flax seeds
- 1 teaspoon (5 g) honey (optional for sweetness)
- Optional: a sprinkle of cinnamon for extra flavor

Instructions:

1. In a bowl, combine the Greek yogurt with ground flax seeds.
2. Optionally, add honey and cinnamon for sweetness and extra flavor.
3. Stir well and enjoy immediately.

Nutritional Information (per serving):

Calories: 200 kcal | Protein: 18 g | Carbohydrates: 10 g | Fat: 9 g | Fiber: 5 g

Adapting for Meal Plans:

- For Fat Loss: Use low-fat or non-fat Greek yogurt to reduce calorie content.
- For Muscle Building: Add an extra scoop of protein powder for more protein.

Turkey Roll-Ups with Cheese

These turkey roll-ups are an easy and protein-rich snack that can be prepared in minutes. Combining lean turkey breast with your choice of cheese, this snack is perfect for a quick, filling option.

Preparation Time: 5 minutes | **Servings**: 2

Ingredients:

- 4 slices (100 g) turkey breast
- 2 slices (30 g) cheese (Swiss, cheddar, or mozzarella)
- 1 tablespoon (15 g) Dijon mustard or mayonnaise (optional for extra flavor)

Instructions:

1. Lay the turkey slices flat and place a slice of cheese on top of each.
2. Roll them up and secure with a toothpick if needed.
3. Serve with a side of mustard or mayonnaise if desired.

Nutritional Information (per serving):

Calories: 200 kcal | Protein: 20 g | Carbohydrates: 2 g | Fat: 12 g | Fiber: 0 g

Adapting for Meal Plans:

- For Fat Loss: Use low-fat cheese or skip the cheese for a lighter version.
- For Muscle Building: Add an extra slice of turkey or cheese for more protein.

Cottage Cheese with Pineapple

This refreshing snack combines creamy cottage cheese with the natural sweetness of pineapple, creating a satisfying high-protein, low-carb option.

Preparation Time: 5 minutes | **Servings:** 1

Ingredients:

- 1/2 cup (120 g) cottage cheese
- 1/4 cup (50 g) pineapple chunks (fresh or canned in juice)
- Optional: a sprinkle of cinnamon or flax seeds for extra flavor and texture

Instructions:

1. In a bowl, top the cottage cheese with pineapple chunks.
2. Optionally, sprinkle with cinnamon or flax seeds for extra texture and flavor.
3. Serve immediately.

Nutritional Information (per serving):

Calories: 180 kcal | Protein: 16 g | Carbohydrates: 10 g | Fat: 8 g | Fiber: 1 g

Adapting for Meal Plans:

- For Fat Loss: Use low-fat cottage cheese for a lighter option.
- For Muscle Building: Add extra cottage cheese for more protein.

Almonds and Dark Chocolate

This snack pairs the crunch of almonds with the rich flavor of dark chocolate, offering a perfect balance of protein, healthy fats, and antioxidants.

Preparation Time: 2 minutes | **Servings**: 1

Ingredients:

- 1/4 cup (30 g) raw almonds
- 2 squares (20 g) dark chocolate (70% cocoa or higher)

Instructions:

1. Combine the almonds and dark chocolate for a quick, satisfying snack.
2. Enjoy immediately or pack for later.

Nutritional Information (per serving):

Calories: 250 kcal | Protein: 6 g | Carbohydrates: 12 g | Fat: 20 g | Fiber: 5 g

Adapting for Meal Plans:

- For Fat Loss: Reduce the portion of dark chocolate or use unsweetened cacao nibs.
- For Muscle Building: Add a spoonful of peanut butter for extra protein and calories.

Mini Caprese Skewers

These bite-sized Caprese skewers combine fresh mozzarella, cherry tomatoes, and basil for a light, refreshing snack that's both delicious and nutritious.

Preparation Time: 5 minutes | **Servings**: 2

Ingredients:

- 8 small fresh mozzarella balls (about 60 g)
- 8 cherry tomatoes
- Fresh basil leaves
- 1 tablespoon (15 ml) olive oil
- 1 teaspoon (5 ml) balsamic vinegar
- Salt and pepper to taste

Instructions:

1. Thread a mozzarella ball, a basil leaf, and a cherry tomato onto small skewers.
2. Drizzle with olive oil and balsamic vinegar. Season with salt and pepper.
3. Serve immediately.

Nutritional Information (per serving):

Calories: 180 kcal | Protein: 8 g | Carbohydrates: 6 g | Fat: 15 g | Fiber: 2 g

Adapting for Meal Plans:

- For Fat Loss: Use light mozzarella to reduce fat content.
- For Muscle Building: Add extra mozzarella or a slice of prosciutto for more protein.

Bell Peppers with Guacamole

This crunchy snack combines fresh bell pepper slices with creamy guacamole for a low-carb, high-protein option that's easy to prepare and full of flavor.

Preparation Time: 5 minutes | **Servings**: 2

Ingredients:

- 1 large bell pepper, sliced
- 1/2 cup (120 g) guacamole (store-bought or homemade)
- Salt and pepper to taste
- Optional: a sprinkle of chili flakes for extra spice

Instructions:

1. Slice the bell pepper into strips and serve with a side of guacamole for dipping.
2. Optionally, season the guacamole with extra salt, pepper, or chili flakes for more flavor. Enjoy immediately.

Nutritional Information (per serving):

Calories: 200 kcal | Protein: 4 g | Carbohydrates: 12 g | Fat: 18 g | Fiber: 6 g

Adapting for Meal Plans:

- For Fat Loss: Use a smaller portion of guacamole or opt for a light version.
- For Muscle Building: Add a boiled egg or a handful of nuts on the side for more protein.

Deviled Eggs with Avocado

These deviled eggs are made with a creamy avocado filling, creating a healthy, high-protein snack that's both delicious and satisfying.

Preparation Time: 10 minutes | **Servings**: 2

Ingredients:

- 4 large eggs, hard-boiled
- 1/2 ripe avocado
- 1 teaspoon (5 ml) lemon juice
- Salt and pepper to taste
- Optional: paprika for garnish

Instructions:

1. Peel the hard-boiled eggs and cut them in half lengthwise. Remove the yolks.
2. In a bowl, mash the avocado with the egg yolks, lemon juice, salt, and pepper until smooth.
3. Spoon the avocado mixture back into the egg whites.
4. Garnish with paprika if desired and serve immediately.

Nutritional Information (per serving):

Calories: 220 kcal | Protein: 12 g | Carbohydrates: 6 g | Fat: 18 g | Fiber: 4 g

Adapting for Meal Plans:

- For Fat Loss: Use fewer egg yolks and a smaller portion of avocado for a lighter version.
- For Muscle Building: Add an extra egg or a side of smoked salmon for more protein.

Smoked Salmon Cucumber Bites

These smoked salmon cucumber bites are light, refreshing, and high in protein, making them a perfect snack or appetizer. They're easy to prepare and packed with flavor.

Preparation Time: 5 minutes | **Servings**: 2

Ingredients:

- 100 g smoked salmon, sliced
- 1 cucumber, sliced into rounds
- 1 tablespoon (15 g) cream cheese (optional)
- Fresh dill for garnish
- Optional: lemon wedges for serving

Instructions:

1. Arrange the cucumber slices on a plate.
2. Top each slice with a small piece of smoked salmon. Optionally, add a dollop of cream cheese.
3. Garnish with fresh dill and serve with lemon wedges if desired.

Nutritional Information (per serving):

Calories: 180 kcal | Protein: 15 g | Carbohydrates: 4 g | Fat: 12 g | Fiber: 1 g

Adapting for Meal Plans:

- For Fat Loss: Skip the cream cheese and use less salmon for a lighter option.
- For Muscle Building: Add extra smoked salmon or serve with a boiled egg for more protein.

Edamame with Sea Salt

Edamame is a simple, high-protein snack that's rich in fiber and nutrients. Steamed and sprinkled with sea salt, it's an easy and healthy option.

Preparation Time: 5 minutes | **Cooking Time:** 5 minutes | **Servings:** 2

Ingredients:

- 1 cup (150 g) edamame, in pods
- 1 teaspoon (5 g) sea salt
- Optional: chili flakes for added spice

Instructions:

1. Steam or boil the edamame for 3-5 minutes until tender.
2. Drain and sprinkle with sea salt and chili flakes if desired.
3. Serve immediately and enjoy by squeezing the beans from the pods.

Nutritional Information (per serving):

Calories: 150 kcal | Protein: 12 g | Carbohydrates: 10 g | Fat: 6 g | Fiber: 5 g

Adapting for Meal Plans:

- For Fat Loss: Use a smaller portion of edamame and less salt to reduce sodium intake.
- For Muscle Building: Serve with a side of nuts or an extra serving of edamame for more protein.

Cucumber and Turkey Slices

This simple and refreshing snack combines the crunch of cucumber with the protein-packed turkey slices for a quick, low-carb option that's easy to prepare and perfect for a healthy bite.

Preparation Time: 5 minutes | **Servings**: 2

Ingredients:

- 1 cucumber, sliced into rounds
- 4 slices (100 g) turkey breast
- 1 tablespoon (15 g) cream cheese or hummus (optional for extra flavor)
- Salt and pepper to taste

Instructions:

1. Spread a small amount of cream cheese or hummus on each cucumber slice (optional).
2. Roll the turkey slices and place them on top of the cucumber rounds.
3. Season with salt and pepper to taste, and serve immediately.

Nutritional Information (per serving):

Calories: 150 kcal | Protein: 20 g | Carbohydrates: 5 g | Fat: 5 g | Fiber: 2 g

Adapting for Meal Plans:

- For Fat Loss: Skip the cream cheese or hummus to reduce fat content.
- For Muscle Building: Add extra turkey or a slice of cheese for more protein.

Protein Muffins with Berries

These high-protein muffins are a delicious and nutritious snack option, perfect for meal prep. Made with protein powder and fresh berries, they're ideal for a post-workout treat or a quick breakfast on the go.

Preparation Time: 10 minutes | **Cooking Time**: 20 minutes | **Servings**: 6 muffins

Ingredients:

- 1 cup (120 g) vanilla protein powder
- 1/2 cup (120 g) almond flour
- 1/2 cup (120 ml) almond milk
- 2 large eggs
- 1/2 cup (75 g) mixed berries (blueberries, raspberries, or strawberries)
- 1 tablespoon (15 ml) honey (optional for sweetness)
- 1 teaspoon (5 g) baking powder
- 1/4 teaspoon (1 g) cinnamon (optional)

Instructions:

1. Preheat the oven to 180°C (350°F) and grease a muffin tin.
2. In a large bowl, mix the protein powder, almond flour, baking powder, and cinnamon.
3. In a separate bowl, whisk together the eggs, almond milk, and honey (if using).
4. Combine the wet and dry ingredients, then gently fold in the berries.
5. Divide the batter evenly among the muffin cups.
6. Bake for 18-20 minutes, or until the muffins are golden and a toothpick inserted in the center comes out clean.
7. Let cool and enjoy. Store in an airtight container for up to 3 days.

Nutritional Information (per muffin):

Calories: 180 kcal | Protein: 12 g | Carbohydrates: 10 g | Fat: 10 g | Fiber: 3 g

Adapting for Meal Plans:

- For Fat Loss: Use less honey or a sugar substitute to reduce calories.
- For Muscle Building: Add extra protein powder or more berries for added nutrition and calories.

Chapter 6: Low-Carb and Protein-Packed Desserts

Staying on track with a low-carb, high-protein lifestyle doesn't mean giving up on sweets! In fact, you can enjoy indulgent desserts that are both delicious and nutritious. The key is to focus on using ingredients that satisfy your sweet tooth while supporting your health and fitness goals.

This section offers a variety of low-carb, protein-rich dessert recipes that are easy to prepare and won't derail your progress. From creamy mousse to rich, chocolatey treats, these desserts will keep you feeling satisfied without the sugar crash.

Let's start with a classic dessert that's light, creamy, and packed with protein: Chocolate Mousse with Greek Yogurt.

Chocolate Mousse with Greek Yogurt

This creamy chocolate mousse is made with Greek yogurt, offering a high-protein, low-carb dessert that feels indulgent but is packed with healthy ingredients.

Preparation Time: 10 minutes | **Chilling Time**: 1 hour | **Servings**: 2

Ingredients:

- 1/2 cup (120 g) plain Greek yogurt (unsweetened)
- 2 tablespoons (15 g) cocoa powder (unsweetened)
- 1 tablespoon (15 ml) almond milk (or any milk of your choice)
- 1 tablespoon (15 g) honey or stevia for sweetness
- 1/4 teaspoon (1 g) vanilla extract
- Optional: dark chocolate shavings or berries for topping

Instructions:

1. In a bowl, mix the Greek yogurt, cocoa powder, almond milk, honey (or stevia), and vanilla extract until smooth and creamy.
2. Divide the mixture into serving cups and refrigerate for at least 1 hour to allow the mousse to set.
3. Optionally, top with dark chocolate shavings or fresh berries before serving.

Nutritional Information (per serving):

Calories: 150 kcal | Protein: 12 g | Carbohydrates: 10 g | Fat: 5 g | Fiber: 2 g

Adapting for Meal Plans:

- For Fat Loss: Use low-fat or non-fat Greek yogurt and a sugar substitute like stevia to reduce calories.
- For Muscle Building: Add an extra scoop of protein powder or top with chopped nuts for more protein and healthy fats.

Chia Seed Pudding with Coconut

This chia seed pudding is a creamy, low-carb dessert rich in fiber and healthy fats. The coconut adds a tropical flavor, making it a satisfying and nutritious sweet treat.

Preparation Time: 5 minutes | **Chilling Time**: 4 hours or overnight | **Servings**: 2

Ingredients:

- 1/4 cup (40 g) chia seeds
- 1 cup (240 ml) coconut milk (light or full-fat)
- 1 tablespoon (15 g) shredded coconut (unsweetened)
- 1 tablespoon (15 ml) honey or a sugar substitute
- 1/2 teaspoon (2 g) vanilla extract
- Optional: fresh berries or extra coconut for topping

Instructions:

1. In a bowl, whisk together the chia seeds, coconut milk, shredded coconut, honey, and vanilla extract until well combined.
2. Divide the mixture into serving cups and refrigerate for at least 4 hours or overnight to allow the pudding to set.
3. Optionally, top with fresh berries or extra shredded coconut before serving.

Nutritional Information (per serving):

Calories: 250 kcal | Protein: 5 g | Carbohydrates: 10 g | Fat: 20 g | Fiber: 8 g

Adapting for Meal Plans:

- For Fat Loss: Use light coconut milk and a sugar substitute to lower calories.
- For Muscle Building: Add a scoop of protein powder or top with nuts for extra protein and calories.

Chocolate Protein Cake with Oats

This rich and moist chocolate protein cake is made with oats and protein powder, offering a healthy, high-protein dessert that satisfies your chocolate cravings without the guilt.

Preparation Time: 10 minutes | **Cooking Time:** 20 minutes | **Servings:** 4

Ingredients:

- 1/2 cup (120 g) rolled oats
- 1/2 cup (120 g) chocolate protein powder
- 2 tablespoons (15 g) cocoa powder (unsweetened)
- 1/4 cup (60 ml) almond milk (or any milk of your choice)
- 2 large eggs
- 1 tablespoon (15 g) honey or stevia for sweetness
- 1 teaspoon (5 g) baking powder
- Optional: dark chocolate chips for topping

Instructions:

1. Preheat the oven to 180°C (350°F) and grease a small baking dish.
2. In a bowl, mix the rolled oats, protein powder, cocoa powder, and baking powder.
3. In a separate bowl, whisk together the eggs, almond milk, and honey (or stevia).
4. Combine the wet and dry ingredients, mixing until smooth. Optionally, fold in dark chocolate chips.
5. Pour the batter into the prepared baking dish and bake for 18-20 minutes, or until a toothpick inserted in the center comes out clean.
6. Let cool before slicing and enjoy.

Nutritional Information (per serving):

Calories: 220 kcal | Protein: 20 g | Carbohydrates: 18 g | Fat: 7 g | Fiber: 4 g

Adapting for Meal Plans:

- For Fat Loss: Use a sugar substitute and skip the dark chocolate chips to reduce calories.
- For Muscle Building: Add extra protein powder or a spoonful of peanut butter for more protein and healthy fats.

Low-Carb Cheesecake

This rich and creamy low-carb cheesecake is a delicious dessert that satisfies your sweet tooth without the sugar. Made with almond flour for the crust and a protein-packed cream cheese filling, it's a perfect high-protein, low-carb treat.

Preparation Time: 15 minutes | **Cooking Time**: 40 minutes | **Servings**: 4

Ingredients:

For the Crust:

- 1/2 cup (60 g) almond flour
- 2 tablespoons (30 g) melted butter
- 1 tablespoon (15 g) sweetener (stevia or erythritol)

For the Filling:

- 200 g cream cheese (full-fat or light)
- 1/4 cup (60 g) Greek yogurt
- 1/4 cup (60 g) sweetener (stevia or erythritol)
- 1 large egg
- 1 teaspoon (5 ml) vanilla extract

Instructions:

1. Preheat the oven to 160°C (320°F) and grease a small springform pan.
2. In a bowl, mix the almond flour, melted butter, and sweetener to form the crust. Press the mixture into the bottom of the springform pan.
3. Bake the crust for 10 minutes, then remove and set aside.
4. In a separate bowl, beat the cream cheese, Greek yogurt, sweetener, egg, and vanilla extract until smooth.
5. Pour the filling over the baked crust and smooth the top.
6. Bake for 30 minutes, or until the cheesecake is set and slightly golden.
7. Let cool before serving. Optionally, top with fresh berries.

Nutritional Information (per serving):

Calories: 280 kcal | Protein: 10 g | Carbohydrates: 6 g | Fat: 24 g | Fiber: 2 g

Adapting for Meal Plans:

- For Fat Loss: Use light cream cheese and Greek yogurt to reduce fat content.
- For Muscle Building: Add a scoop of protein powder to the filling for extra protein.

Almond Flour Brownies

These rich and fudgy brownies are made with almond flour, offering a delicious low-carb, high-protein dessert that satisfies your chocolate cravings while keeping carbs low.

Preparation Time: 10 minutes | **Cooking Time**: 20 minutes | **Servings**: 6

Ingredients:

- 1/2 cup (120 g) almond flour
- 1/4 cup (30 g) cocoa powder (unsweetened)
- 1/4 cup (60 ml) almond milk (or any milk of your choice)
- 1/4 cup (60 ml) coconut oil (melted)
- 1/4 cup (60 g) sweetener (stevia or erythritol)
- 2 large eggs
- 1 teaspoon (5 g) baking powder
- 1/2 teaspoon (2 g) vanilla extract
- Optional: dark chocolate chips for topping

Instructions:

1. Preheat the oven to 180°C (350°F) and grease a small baking pan.
2. In a bowl, mix the almond flour, cocoa powder, and baking powder.
3. In a separate bowl, whisk together the eggs, almond milk, coconut oil, sweetener, and vanilla extract.
4. Combine the wet and dry ingredients until smooth. Optionally, fold in dark chocolate chips.
5. Pour the batter into the prepared baking pan and bake for 18-20 minutes, or until a toothpick inserted in the center comes out clean.
6. Let cool before slicing and enjoy.

Nutritional Information (per serving):

Calories: 220 kcal | Protein: 6 g | Carbohydrates: 10 g | Fat: 18 g | Fiber: 4 g

Adapting for Meal Plans:

- For Fat Loss: Use a sugar substitute and reduce the portion of coconut oil to lower calories.
- For Muscle Building: Add a scoop of protein powder for extra protein.

Lemon Protein Bars

These lemon protein bars are tangy, refreshing, and packed with protein. They're a perfect snack or dessert that's low in carbs but high in flavor and nutrition.

Preparation Time: 10 minutes | **Chilling Time**: 1 hour | **Servings**: 4 bars

Ingredients:

- 1/2 cup (120 g) vanilla protein powder
- 1/2 cup (120 g) almond flour
- 1 tablespoon (15 ml) lemon juice
- 1 tablespoon (15 g) honey or stevia
- 1/4 cup (60 ml) almond milk
- 1 teaspoon (5 ml) lemon zest

Instructions:

1. In a bowl, mix the protein powder, almond flour, lemon juice, honey, almond milk, and lemon zest until smooth.
2. Press the mixture into a small pan or dish and refrigerate for at least 1 hour.
3. Once firm, cut into bars and enjoy. Store in the fridge for up to a week.

Nutritional Information (per bar):

Calories: 180 kcal | Protein: 12 g | Carbohydrates: 8 g | Fat: 10 g | Fiber: 3 g

Adapting for Meal Plans:

- For Fat Loss: Use a sugar substitute like stevia to reduce calories.
- For Muscle Building: Add extra protein powder or top with almonds for more protein and healthy fats.

Low-Carb Chocolate Chip Cookies

These low-carb chocolate chip cookies are a healthier twist on the classic treat. Made with almond flour and dark chocolate chips, they're a delicious high-protein snack or dessert.

Preparation Time: 10 minutes | **Cooking Time**: 12 minutes | **Servings**: 6

Ingredients:

- 1 cup (120 g) almond flour
- 1/4 cup (30 g) dark chocolate chips (sugar-free or 70% cocoa)
- 1/4 cup (60 g) coconut oil (melted)
- 1/4 cup (60 g) sweetener (stevia or erythritol)
- 1 large egg
- 1/2 teaspoon (2 g) vanilla extract
- 1/2 teaspoon (2 g) baking soda

Instructions:

1. Preheat the oven to 180°C (350°F) and line a baking sheet with parchment paper.
2. In a bowl, mix the almond flour, baking soda, and sweetener.
3. In a separate bowl, whisk together the egg, coconut oil, and vanilla extract.
4. Combine the wet and dry ingredients, then fold in the dark chocolate chips.
5. Scoop small balls of dough onto the baking sheet and flatten slightly.
6. Bake for 10-12 minutes, or until golden brown. Let cool and enjoy.

Nutritional Information (per serving):

Calories: 160 kcal | Protein: 4 g | Carbohydrates: 8 g | Fat: 14 g | Fiber: 3 g

Adapting for Meal Plans:

- For Fat Loss: Use a sugar substitute and reduce the amount of chocolate chips.
- For Muscle Building: Add a scoop of protein powder to the dough for more protein.

Raspberry Protein Ice Cream

This refreshing raspberry protein ice cream is made with simple, healthy ingredients and offers a high-protein, low-carb dessert that's perfect for hot days or a post-workout treat.

Preparation Time: 5 minutes | **Freezing Time**: 2 hours | **Servings**: 2

Ingredients:

- 1/2 cup (120 g) vanilla protein powder
- 1 cup (150 g) frozen raspberries
- 1/2 cup (120 ml) unsweetened almond milk
- 1 tablespoon (15 g) sweetener (optional)

Instructions:

1. In a blender, combine the protein powder, frozen raspberries, almond milk, and sweetener.
2. Blend until smooth and creamy.
3. Transfer to a freezer-safe container and freeze for at least 2 hours.
4. Scoop and serve immediately.

Nutritional Information (per serving):

Calories: 150 kcal | Protein: 15 g | Carbohydrates: 10 g | Fat: 4 g | Fiber: 5 g

Adapting for Meal Plans:

- For Fat Loss: Use less sweetener or a sugar substitute to reduce calories.
- For Muscle Building: Add extra protein powder or serve with a handful of nuts for more protein.

Peanut Butter Protein Fudge

This creamy peanut butter protein fudge is a decadent, high-protein dessert that's easy to make and perfect for satisfying your sweet tooth while staying on track with your fitness goals.

Preparation Time: 5 minutes | **Chilling Time**: 1 hour | **Servings**: 4

Ingredients:

- 1/2 cup (120 g) peanut butter (or almond butter)
- 1/4 cup (60 g) vanilla protein powder
- 1 tablespoon (15 ml) coconut oil (melted)
- 1 tablespoon (15 g) honey or stevia for sweetness
- Optional: dark chocolate chips for topping

Instructions:

1. In a bowl, mix the peanut butter, protein powder, coconut oil, and honey until smooth.
2. Press the mixture into a small pan or dish and top with dark chocolate chips if desired.
3. Chill in the fridge for at least 1 hour until firm.
4. Slice into small squares and enjoy.

Nutritional Information (per serving):

Calories: 220 kcal | Protein: 12 g | Carbohydrates: 8 g | Fat: 18 g | Fiber: 3 g

Adapting for Meal Plans:

- For Fat Loss: Use powdered peanut butter and a sugar substitute to reduce fat and calories.
- For Muscle Building: Add extra protein powder for more protein.

Vanilla Protein Pudding

This creamy vanilla protein pudding is a simple, high-protein dessert that's quick to prepare and perfect for satisfying sweet cravings without the sugar.

Preparation Time: 5 minutes | **Chilling Time**: 1 hour | **Servings**: 2

Ingredients:

- 1/2 cup (120 g) vanilla protein powder
- 1 cup (240 ml) unsweetened almond milk
- 1 tablespoon (15 g) chia seeds
- 1 teaspoon (5 ml) vanilla extract
- 1 tablespoon (15 g) sweetener (optional)

Instructions:

1. In a bowl, whisk together the protein powder, almond milk, chia seeds, vanilla extract, and sweetener.
2. Pour into serving cups and refrigerate for at least 1 hour until set.
3. Serve chilled and enjoy.

Nutritional Information (per serving):

Calories: 180 kcal | Protein: 20 g | Carbohydrates: 6 g | Fat: 8 g | Fiber: 4 g

Adapting for Meal Plans:

- For Fat Loss: Use less sweetener or a sugar substitute to reduce calories.
- For Muscle Building: Add more protein powder or top with chopped nuts for extra protein.

Chapter 7: Meal Prep Tips and Essential Tools

Meal prepping is one of the most effective ways to stay on track with a low-carb, high-protein lifestyle. By preparing your meals in advance, you eliminate the stress of last-minute decisions and reduce the temptation to reach for unhealthy options. Plus, it saves time and ensures that you always have nutritious, delicious food ready to go.

In this chapter, we'll cover the essential tools you need to get started with meal prep, as well as some time-saving tips that will make the process more efficient. Whether you're new to meal prepping or looking to streamline your routine, these suggestions will help you stay organized and focused on your health goals.

Let's dive into the tools that will make your meal prep routine easier and more efficient.

Essential Meal Prep Tools

To make meal prep efficient and enjoyable, having the right tools is key. You don't need a kitchen full of gadgets, but investing in a few quality items can make all the difference. Here are some essential tools that will help you save time, stay organized, and create delicious low-carb, high-protein meals with ease:

1. Meal Prep Containers

Sturdy, airtight containers are essential for storing your prepped meals. Look for ones that are BPA-free, microwave-safe, and have compartments to separate ingredients. Glass containers are a great option if you prefer a more durable and eco-friendly choice.

2. Food Scale

A digital food scale is crucial for accurate portioning, especially when it comes to managing your protein and carb intake. It ensures that you're getting the right amounts of each macronutrient to meet your goals, whether you're focusing on fat loss or muscle building.

3. Measuring Cups and Spoons

These are indispensable for measuring ingredients like protein powder, flours, and liquids. They help maintain accuracy in your recipes and ensure consistent portion sizes.

4. Sharp Knives

A good set of sharp kitchen knives makes chopping vegetables, meats, and other ingredients faster and safer. A quality chef's knife and a paring knife are must-haves in any kitchen.

5. Blender or Food Processor

Whether you're making smoothies, protein shakes, or blending sauces and dressings, a reliable blender or food processor is a game changer. It also helps with prepping items like cauliflower rice or pureeing soups.

6. Slow Cooker or Instant Pot

These tools are perfect for preparing large batches of protein-rich meals like stews, soups, and roasts with minimal effort. You can set them up in the morning and come home to a fully cooked meal.

7. Non-Stick Pans

Investing in a good set of non-stick pans makes cooking lean proteins like chicken, eggs, and fish much easier, as they reduce the need for excessive oil and ensure easy cleanup.

8. Cutting Boards

Have separate cutting boards for vegetables and proteins to avoid cross-contamination. Look for durable, dishwasher-safe options for easy cleaning.

With these essential tools, you'll be well-equipped to start your meal prep routine efficiently and with confidence.

Time-Saving Tips for Meal Prep

Meal prepping doesn't have to be a time-consuming task. With a few smart strategies, you can streamline the process and make it part of your weekly routine without feeling overwhelmed. Here are some time-saving tips to help you stay on track with your low-carb, high-protein lifestyle while minimizing time spent in the kitchen:

1. Plan Your Meals in Advance

The key to successful meal prep is having a plan. Before you start cooking, decide what meals you'll prepare for the week. Use the recipes from this book to build a balanced menu based on your goals, whether it's fat loss or muscle building. Having a clear plan prevents last-minute decisions and ensures you're always ready with healthy meals.

2. Batch Cook Your Proteins

Cook larger quantities of lean proteins like chicken, turkey, or beef at once. You can roast or grill a batch of chicken breasts, cook ground turkey, or make a large stew in a slow cooker. Portion out the cooked protein into containers and use it in various meals throughout the week.

3. Chop Vegetables in Bulk

Instead of chopping vegetables every time you cook, prep all your veggies at once. Store them in airtight containers, ready to be added to salads, stir-fries, or as sides. You can also use pre-cut or frozen vegetables for added convenience.

4. Use the Freezer Wisely

Freeze meals or individual ingredients like cooked proteins, soups, and sauces. This way, you'll always have something ready to go on busy days. Label everything with the date to avoid confusion and rotate older meals to the front of your freezer.

5. Cook One-Pot or Sheet-Pan Meals

One-pot meals and sheet-pan dinners are excellent for meal prep because they minimize the number of dishes you need to clean. Simply combine your proteins, vegetables, and seasonings in one pan, cook, and divide into portions for the week.

6. Prepare Breakfast and Snacks in Advance

To make mornings easier, prepare your high-protein breakfasts, like overnight oats, chia puddings, or egg muffins, in advance. Having protein-packed snacks like boiled eggs, homemade protein bars, or pre-cut veggies ready will also help curb hunger between meals.

7. Use Multi-Tasking Tools

Appliances like slow cookers, Instant Pots, or rice cookers can cook your proteins, grains, or vegetables while you focus on other tasks. This allows you to prepare multiple components of your meals at the same time, saving you hours in the kitchen.

8. Label and Organize Your Meals

Label each meal or container with the date and type of meal. This helps you keep track of what's in the fridge and ensures you're eating your meals before they spoil. It also helps you organize your meal plan efficiently.

By implementing these time-saving tips, you'll make meal prep a simple, manageable part of your routine, ensuring you always have healthy, low-carb, high-protein meals ready to support your goals.

Chapter 8: 30-Day Meal Plan Guide

Now that you've got a collection of delicious low-carb, high-protein recipes and meal prep strategies, it's time to put it all together with a structured plan. Whether your goal is fat loss, muscle building, or simply maintaining a balanced and healthy lifestyle, following a meal plan can provide the guidance and consistency you need to see real results.

This 30-day meal plan is designed to help you stay on track, offering a balanced mix of proteins, healthy fats, and low-carb vegetables. Each day is structured to provide optimal nutrition, keeping you satisfied and energized while supporting your fitness goals. The plan is flexible and can be adapted based on your individual needs, preferences, and calorie requirements.

In this chapter, we'll break down:

- How to structure your daily meal plan for success.
- How to balance your macronutrients (proteins, fats, and carbs) effectively.
- Guidelines for portion control.
- A detailed calorie and macronutrient chart to guide you through the 30 days.

Let's start with the structure of the daily meal plan and how to use it to meet your goals.

Structuring the Daily Meal Plan

A well-structured meal plan provides consistency and helps you reach your goals by ensuring that each meal is balanced and nutrient-dense. For this 30-day meal plan, we've designed a flexible structure that can be adapted based on whether your focus is on fat loss or muscle building.

Here's how to structure your meals for each day:

1. Breakfast

Start your day with a high-protein breakfast that keeps you full and energized. Choose from options like omelets, protein smoothies, or chia puddings. Aim for a balance of lean protein, healthy fats, and low-carb vegetables or fruits. This will kickstart your metabolism and stabilize your blood sugar levels throughout the morning.

2. Lunch

For lunch, prioritize lean proteins like chicken, turkey, or fish, paired with non-starchy vegetables such as spinach, broccoli, or zucchini. Include a source of healthy fats, like avocado or olive oil, to keep you satisfied until your next meal. Depending on your goals, you can add complex carbs like sweet potatoes or quinoa for muscle building.

3. Dinner

Dinner should be light yet satisfying. Stick with a protein-rich option, like grilled salmon, chicken, or beef, along with a generous portion of vegetables. If your focus is fat loss, keep the carbohydrates low. If muscle building is your goal, feel free to add a side of complex carbs like brown rice or roasted root vegetables.

4. Snacks

Snacks are optional but can help keep you on track if you feel hungry between meals. High-protein, low-carb options like boiled eggs, Greek yogurt, or mixed nuts are great for keeping your hunger in check while providing essential nutrients.

5. Post-Workout Meals (Optional)

If you're including workouts as part of your routine, your post-workout meal should be rich in protein and moderate in carbohydrates. Protein shakes, chicken and rice, or eggs with avocado are excellent choices for replenishing your muscles and supporting recovery.

6. Hydration

Throughout the day, stay hydrated by drinking plenty of water. Aim for at least 8 glasses a day. You can also include herbal teas or black coffee, but avoid sugary drinks that can derail your progress.

7. Flexibility and Adjustments

Each individual has different needs, so feel free to adjust the portions or types of meals based on your activity level, body composition goals, and preferences. You can refer to the macronutrient chart later in this chapter to ensure your meals align with your specific objectives.

Balancing Protein and Carbohydrates

One of the key factors in achieving your fitness goals—whether it's fat loss, muscle building, or maintaining your current weight—is striking the right balance between protein and carbohydrates. This balance affects how your body burns fat, builds muscle, and maintains energy levels throughout the day. Let's break down how to achieve this balance based on your specific goals.

1. Protein: Your Main Fuel for Muscle and Satiety

Protein is the foundation of your meal plan. It supports muscle growth, repair, and recovery while keeping you feeling full and satisfied. For both fat loss and muscle building, it's essential to consume adequate protein at every meal.

Daily Protein Target:

- For Fat Loss: Aim for 1.6–2.2 grams of protein per kilogram of body weight. This helps maintain muscle mass while in a calorie deficit.
- For Muscle Building: Target 2.2–2.7 grams of protein per kilogram of body weight. Increased protein intake supports muscle recovery and growth after workouts.

Protein Sources:

- Lean meats like chicken, turkey, and beef.
- Fish and seafood, such as salmon, tuna, and shrimp.
- Eggs and egg whites.
- Dairy products like Greek yogurt and cottage cheese.
- Plant-based proteins, including tofu, tempeh, and protein powders.

2. Carbohydrates: Controlled Intake for Energy

Carbohydrates are the body's primary energy source, but in a low-carb, high-protein plan, we aim to moderate carb intake to encourage fat burning and maintain steady energy levels without sugar spikes.

Daily Carb Target:

- For Fat Loss: Keep carbohydrates at 50–100 grams per day. This level is low enough to promote fat loss while providing enough fuel for daily activities.
- For Muscle Building: Increase carb intake to 150–250 grams per day. Carbohydrates play a crucial role in fueling workouts and supporting muscle recovery.

Carbohydrate Sources:

- Low-carb vegetables, such as spinach, broccoli, cauliflower, and zucchini.
- Berries and other low-sugar fruits, like strawberries, blueberries, and raspberries.
- Complex carbohydrates for muscle building, including sweet potatoes, quinoa, and brown rice (for those with higher carb needs).

3. **Timing Your Carbs**

For fat loss, the best time to consume carbohydrates is around your workouts, as your body will use them efficiently for energy and recovery. If you're building muscle, you can include carbs at each meal, focusing on complex, slow-digesting options to keep energy levels stable.

Portion Guidelines

Understanding portion control is crucial for staying on track with your low-carb, high-protein plan. The right portion sizes will help you manage calorie intake, ensure you're getting enough protein, and keep your meals balanced without over- or under-eating.

Here's a simple guide to help you measure your portions without needing to count every calorie:

1. **Protein Portions**

For optimal results, your meals should be built around protein. A good portion size for most people is between 100–150 grams (3.5–5 oz) of cooked lean protein per meal, which provides about 25–35 grams of protein.

Easy Measurement Tip:

A portion of protein (like chicken, fish, or beef) should be roughly the size of the palm of your hand.

2. **Carbohydrate Portions**

Carbohydrates should be kept moderate, especially if your goal is fat loss. For low-carb meals, aim for 1/2 to 1 cup (50–100 grams) of cooked complex carbohydrates (such as quinoa, sweet potatoes, or brown rice) or a larger portion of non-starchy vegetables (about 1–2 cups).

Easy Measurement Tip:

A portion of carbs (like quinoa or sweet potatoes) should be about the size of your cupped hand, while vegetables should take up half your plate.

3. **Fat Portions**

Healthy fats are an important part of your meal plan, helping you stay full and supporting your metabolism. Include about 1–2 tablespoons (15–30 grams) of healthy fats per meal, such as olive oil, avocado, or nuts.

Easy Measurement Tip:

A portion of fat (like olive oil or nut butter) should be about the size of your thumb.

4. **Vegetables**

Non-starchy vegetables should make up a large part of your plate. Aim for at least 1–2 cups (150–300 grams) of vegetables with each meal. They are nutrient-dense, low in calories, and high in fiber, which will help you feel full and satisfied.

Easy Measurement Tip:

A portion of vegetables should fill about half your plate, or be roughly two fist-sized portions.

5. **Snacks**

For snacks, keep portions moderate and protein-focused. Ideal snack portions include 1/2 cup (120 g) of Greek yogurt, a handful of nuts, or 2 hard-boiled eggs.

Easy Measurement Tip:

Snacks should be around 100–200 calories and high in protein to keep you full until your next meal.

6. **Adjusting Portions Based on Goals**
   - For Fat Loss: Stick to smaller portion sizes, especially for fats and carbohydrates. Prioritize vegetables and lean proteins to create a calorie deficit while staying full.
   - For Muscle Building: Increase your portion sizes, especially for protein and complex carbohydrates. This will provide your body with the extra fuel and nutrients needed for muscle growth and recovery.

By following these portion guidelines, you'll be able to create balanced meals that align with your goals, whether it's fat loss, muscle building, or maintaining a healthy lifestyle.

Calorie and Macronutrient Chart

To help you better understand how much you're consuming each day and ensure you're meeting your specific goals, here's a calorie and macronutrient chart that breaks down common foods used in this meal plan. Use this guide to track your daily intake of calories, protein, carbs, and fats.

Lean Proteins

Food	Serving Size	Calories	Protein (g)	Carbs (g)	Fat (g)
Chicken Breast (cooked)	100 g (3.5 oz)	165	31	0	4
Turkey Breast (cooked)	100 g (3.5 oz)	135	30	0	1
Salmon (cooked)	100 g (3.5 oz)	206	22	0	13
Eggs (whole)	1 large egg	70	6	1	5
Egg Whites	100 g (3.5 oz)	52	11	1	0
Tofu (firm)	100 g (3.5 oz)	76	8	2	4
Cottage Cheese	1/2 cup (120 g)	110	12	5	5

Low-Carb Vegetables

Food	Serving Size	Calories	Protein (g)	Carbs (g)	Fat (g)
Spinach (cooked)	100 g (3.5 oz)	23	3	4	0
Broccoli (cooked)	100 g (3.5 oz)	55	3	11	0
Zucchini (cooked)	100 g (3.5 oz)	17	1	3	0
Bell Peppers	100 g (3.5 oz)	31	1	6	0
Cauliflower (cooked)	100 g (3.5 oz)	25	2	5	0
Kale (raw)	100 g (3.5 oz)	35	3	7	1

Healthy Fats

Food	Serving Size	Calories	Protein (g)	Carbs (g)	Fat (g)
Avocado	100 g (3.5 oz)	160	2	9	15
Olive Oil	1 tablespoon (15 ml)	120	0	0	14
Almonds	1/4 cup (30 g)	170	6	6	15
Peanut Butter	2 tablespoons (30 g)	190	8	6	16
Chia Seeds	2 tablespoons (30 g)	137	4	12	9
Flax Seeds	1 tablespoon (15 g)	55	2	3	4

Complex Carbohydrates

Food	Serving Size	Calories	Protein (g)	Carbs (g)	Fat (g)
Sweet Potatoes (cooked)	100 g (3.5 oz)	86	2	20	0
Quinoa (cooked)	100 g (3.5 oz)	120	4	21	2
Brown Rice (cooked)	100 g (3.5 oz)	110	2	23	0
Oats (cooked)	1/2 cup (40 g)	150	5	27	3
Lentils (cooked)	100 g (3.5 oz)	116	9	20	0

By using this chart, you can adjust your meals to match your daily calorie and macronutrient goals, ensuring that you're fueling your body in the right way for fat loss, muscle building, or maintenance.

30-Day Meal Plan for Fat Loss and Muscle Building

This 30-day meal plan is designed to help you stay consistent with your low-carb, high-protein lifestyle. Whether your goal is fat loss or muscle building, this plan provides a balanced approach with easy-to-follow recipes. Each day includes breakfast, lunch, dinner, and a snack, with simple adjustments based on your specific goals.

Follow the plan as outlined, or feel free to swap out meals depending on your preferences. Remember, consistency is key, so having your meals planned out in advance will help you stay on track and achieve lasting results. Adjust portion sizes and ingredients as needed to match your activity level and dietary needs.

Day	Breakfast	Lunch	Snack	Dinner
Day 1	Spinach & Feta High-Protein Omelette	Grilled Chicken Salad with Avocado	Greek Yogurt with Flax Seeds	Baked Salmon with Asparagus
Day 2	Peanut Butter Protein Smoothie	Turkey Wrap with Spinach	Almonds and Dark Chocolate	Grilled Steak with Roasted Vegetables
Day 3	Cottage Cheese with Pineapple	Chicken Stir-Fry with Cauliflower Rice	Hard-Boiled Eggs with Sunflower Seeds	Chicken Fajitas with Peppers and Onions
Day 4	Protein Pancakes with Fresh Berries	Tuna Salad with Avocado	Turkey Roll-Ups with Cheese	Baked Tilapia with Spinach
Day 5	Greek Yogurt with Berries and Nuts	Grilled Pork Chops with Asparagus	Homemade Protein Bars	Shrimp Scampi with Zoodles
Day 6	Peanut Butter Protein Shake	Beef Stir-Fry with Vegetables	Cottage Cheese with Pineapple	Chicken Alfredo with Zucchini Noodles
Day 7	Almond Flour Protein Muffins with Berries	Grilled Chicken Salad with Avocado	Hummus and Celery Sticks	Baked Salmon with Spinach

Day 8	Spinach & Feta High-Protein Omelette	Turkey and Cheese Roll-Ups	Greek Yogurt with Flax Seeds	Grilled Steak with Asparagus
Day 9	Peanut Butter Protein Smoothie	Tuna Salad with Avocado	Almonds and Dark Chocolate	Shrimp Scampi with Zoodles
Day 10	Cottage Cheese with Pineapple	Chicken Stir-Fry with Vegetables	Hard-Boiled Eggs with Sunflower Seeds	Grilled Pork Chops with Asparagus
Day 11	Protein Pancakes with Fresh Berries	Grilled Chicken Salad with Avocado	Turkey Roll-Ups with Cheese	Baked Tilapia with Spinach
Day 12	Greek Yogurt with Berries and Nuts	Beef Stir-Fry with Vegetables	Homemade Protein Bars	Grilled Steak with Roasted Vegetables
Day 13	Peanut Butter Protein Shake	Grilled Chicken Salad with Avocado	Hummus and Celery Sticks	Chicken Alfredo with Zucchini Noodles
Day 14	Almond Flour Protein Muffins with Berries	Tuna Salad with Avocado	Greek Yogurt with Flax Seeds	Shrimp Scampi with Zoodles
Day 15	Spinach & Feta High-Protein Omelette	Grilled Pork Chops with Asparagus	Cottage Cheese with Pineapple	Baked Salmon with Asparagus
Day 16	Peanut Butter Protein Smoothie	Turkey Wrap with Spinach	Almonds and Dark Chocolate	Grilled Steak with Roasted Vegetables
Day 17	Cottage Cheese with Pineapple	Chicken Stir-Fry with Cauliflower Rice	Hard-Boiled Eggs with Sunflower Seeds	Chicken Fajitas with Peppers and Onions

Day 18	Protein Pancakes with Fresh Berries	Tuna Salad with Avocado	Turkey Roll-Ups with Cheese	Baked Tilapia with Spinach
Day 19	Greek Yogurt with Berries and Nuts	Grilled Pork Chops with Asparagus	Homemade Protein Bars	Shrimp Scampi with Zoodles
Day 20	Peanut Butter Protein Shake	Beef Stir-Fry with Vegetables	Cottage Cheese with Pineapple	Chicken Alfredo with Zucchini Noodles
Day 21	Almond Flour Protein Muffins with Berries	Grilled Chicken Salad with Avocado	Hummus and Celery Sticks	Baked Salmon with Spinach
Day 22	Spinach & Feta High-Protein Omelette	Turkey and Cheese Roll-Ups	Greek Yogurt with Flax Seeds	Grilled Steak with Asparagus
Day 23	Peanut Butter Protein Smoothie	Tuna Salad with Avocado	Almonds and Dark Chocolate	Shrimp Scampi with Zoodles
Day 24	Cottage Cheese with Pineapple	Chicken Stir-Fry with Vegetables	Hard-Boiled Eggs with Sunflower Seeds	Grilled Pork Chops with Asparagus
Day 25	Protein Pancakes with Fresh Berries	Grilled Chicken Salad with Avocado	Turkey Roll-Ups with Cheese	Baked Tilapia with Spinach
Day 26	Greek Yogurt with Berries and Nuts	Beef Stir-Fry with Vegetables	Homemade Protein Bars	Grilled Steak with Roasted Vegetables
Day 27	Peanut Butter Protein Shake	Grilled Chicken Salad with Avocado	Hummus and Celery Sticks	Chicken Alfredo with Zucchini Noodles

Day 28	Almond Flour Protein Muffins with Berries	Tuna Salad with Avocado	Greek Yogurt with Flax Seeds	Shrimp Scampi with Zoodles
Day 29	Spinach & Feta High-Protein Omelette	Grilled Pork Chops with Asparagus	Cottage Cheese with Pineapple	Baked Salmon with Asparagus
Day 30	Peanut Butter Protein Smoothie	Turkey Wrap with Spinach	Almonds and Dark Chocolate	Grilled Steak with Roasted Vegetables

Chapter 9: Maintaining Success and Next Goals

You've come a long way on your journey toward a healthier, stronger version of yourself, but this is just the beginning. Adopting a low-carb, high-protein lifestyle may seem like a significant commitment at first, but with the right strategies, tools, and recipes, it becomes a sustainable and enjoyable way of living.

This book has equipped you with:

- Delicious, protein-packed recipes designed to support your goals.
- Meal prep tips and essential tools to help you stay organized and save time.
- A comprehensive 30-day meal plan to keep you on track, whether you're focused on fat loss or building muscle.

Now that you've gained the knowledge and skills to make these changes, it's time to focus on maintaining your progress and continuing to refine your approach as your goals evolve. In this chapter, we'll discuss how to sustain your success in the long term and how to adapt your meal plan to meet new objectives as they arise.

Let's dive into the steps that will help you maintain your results and stay motivated for the future.

Maintaining Results Long-Term

Reaching your fitness and health goals is an accomplishment, but maintaining those results is where the real challenge begins. The good news is that by sticking to the core principles of a low-carb, high-protein lifestyle, you can keep your progress steady without feeling deprived or overwhelmed.

Here are some key strategies to help you maintain your results long-term:

1. Stay Consistent, But Flexible

Consistency is the foundation of long-term success. Keep following the basic structure of your meal plan—focusing on high-protein, low-carb meals—but allow yourself flexibility. Occasional treats or higher-carb meals can fit into your lifestyle as long as they don't become the norm. Flexibility prevents burnout and keeps your diet sustainable in the long run.

2. Monitor Your Progress

Even after reaching your initial goals, it's important to keep track of your progress. Regularly monitor your weight, body measurements, or fitness performance to ensure that you're staying on track. If you notice changes, such as weight gain or muscle loss, you can quickly adjust your meal plan or activity levels accordingly.

3. Prioritize Protein in Every Meal

Protein should remain the focus of your diet. It keeps you full, supports muscle maintenance, and prevents overeating. As you transition from a focused fat loss or muscle building phase into maintenance, ensure that each meal contains a solid source of lean protein to keep your metabolism active and your body in optimal shape.

4. Incorporate Variety

One of the challenges of maintaining results long-term is avoiding boredom. Make sure to incorporate a variety of proteins, vegetables, and healthy fats in your meals. Try new recipes from this book, experiment with different flavors, and keep your meals exciting. Variety not only keeps you engaged but also ensures you get a wide range of nutrients.

5. **Stay Active**

While your meal plan is the cornerstone of your results, maintaining an active lifestyle is just as important. Aim for regular physical activity, whether it's strength training, cardio, or a combination of both. Staying active helps you maintain your metabolism, supports muscle mass, and enhances overall well-being.

6. **Listen to Your Body**

As your goals and lifestyle change over time, so will your body's needs. If you're feeling fatigued, constantly hungry, or notice changes in your energy levels, it might be time to adjust your portion sizes or macronutrient balance. Your body will tell you what it needs—pay attention to these signals and adapt as necessary.

By following these principles, you can maintain the progress you've worked hard to achieve while continuing to enjoy the benefits of a low-carb, high-protein lifestyle.

Adapting Your Meal Plan for Future Goals

As you continue on your health journey, your goals may shift. Whether you want to maintain your current physique, focus on gaining muscle, or shed a few extra pounds, it's important to adjust your meal plan to align with your evolving needs.

Here's how to adapt your low-carb, high-protein plan for different phases of your fitness journey:

1. **For Fat Loss**

If your goal shifts back to fat loss, return to a more structured low-carb approach. Keep your daily carbohydrate intake between 50-100 grams and prioritize lean proteins and plenty of non-starchy vegetables. Reducing calorie-dense fats and minimizing carbohydrate intake will help your body burn fat more efficiently.

Key Adjustments:

- Decrease portion sizes for carbohydrates and fats.
- Focus on leaner protein sources like chicken, turkey, and fish.
- Increase non-starchy vegetables to create volume without adding excess calories.
- Include protein-rich snacks to maintain satiety without overconsuming calories.

2. **For Muscle Building**

When your goal is to build muscle, you'll need to increase both your protein and calorie intake to support growth. This involves consuming more complex carbohydrates and healthy fats alongside protein to fuel workouts and muscle recovery. Aim for 150-250 grams of carbohydrates per day to support higher energy needs, especially around your workouts.

Key Adjustments:

- Increase portion sizes for proteins and complex carbohydrates.
- Incorporate more calorie-dense foods like nuts, avocados, and whole grains.
- Time carbohydrates around your workouts to fuel performance and aid recovery.
- Maintain a high-protein intake, with at least 2.2-2.7 grams of protein per kilogram of body weight.

3. **For Maintenance**

If you've reached your goal and want to maintain your results, aim for balance. A moderate intake of carbohydrates, fats, and proteins will help you maintain your weight while enjoying flexibility in your diet. Your calorie needs will be slightly higher than during fat loss but not as high as in muscle-building phases.

Key Adjustments:

- Adjust carbohydrate intake to 100-150 grams per day, depending on your activity level.
- Continue focusing on high-protein meals, but allow for more flexibility with fats and carbohydrates.
- Include a variety of food sources to ensure you're getting a wide range of nutrients.
- Stay active to maintain your metabolism and overall fitness.

4. **Tracking and Adjusting Over Time**

Your meal plan is not static—it should evolve with you. Keep track of how your body responds to changes in your diet. If you notice weight creeping back on, reduce your carb and fat intake slightly. If you're struggling to gain muscle, increase your calorie intake with more protein and complex carbohydrates. Always adjust based on your progress and how your body feels.

By making these adjustments, you'll be able to continuously adapt your low-carb, high-protein plan to support your health and fitness goals at every stage of your journey.

Conclusion

Thank You for Choosing This Book!

Dear Reader,

Thank you so much for purchasing **The Ultimate Low-Carb High-Protein Cookbook for Beginners**. I truly appreciate you choosing this book to support your health journey, and I hope the recipes and meal plans have been helpful in reaching your goals. Whether you're focusing on fat loss, building lean muscle, or just maintaining a healthier lifestyle, I'm thrilled to be a part of your process.

Exclusive Bonuses Just for You!

As a special thank you for your support, I'm excited to offer you these three exclusive bonuses:

1. **Weekly Shopping List**

A detailed shopping list that aligns with your meal plan, tailored to help you stay organized and make grocery shopping a breeze. Whether you're aiming for fat loss or muscle gain, this list will simplify your meal prep process.

2. **1-Hour Meal Prep Plan**

With just one hour in the kitchen, you can prepare meals for the entire week! This meal prep guide will show you how to batch-cook key ingredients, so you can save time while staying on track with your nutritional goals.

3. **High-Protein Snacks for Every Occasion**

Never be stuck without a healthy option! This guide is packed with snack ideas that are quick to prepare, delicious, and high in protein—perfect for any time of day, whether you need a pre-workout boost or a post-workout recovery.

To access these **free bonuses**, simply scan the QR code below and download them directly to your device!

Bonus 1	Bonus 2	Bonus 3

Loved the Book? Leave a Review!

If you enjoyed the book and found the recipes helpful, I would be incredibly grateful if you could leave a review. Your feedback helps me improve and also helps other readers discover the book and start their own journey toward better health.

Thank you again for choosing this book. I wish you continued success and many delicious meals ahead!

With gratitude,

Liam D. Sterling

Printed in Great Britain
by Amazon